WEAR PINK, LOVE YOURSELF

ETHAN WALKER

authorHOUSE

AuthorHouse™ UK
1663 Liberty Drive
Bloomington, IN 47403 USA
www.authorhouse.co.uk
Phone: 0800 047 8203 (Domestic TFN)
+44 1908 723714 (International)

Published by AuthorHouse 11/28/2019

ISBN: 978-1-7283-9641-5 (sc)
ISBN: 978-1-7283-9640-8 (e)

CONTENTS

BEFORE LEAVING ALBANIA

I remember seeing the most beautiful view when I was 5 years old. The river, the hills, and the sky became orange before sunset. At that moment, I asked my first philosophical question: *Is this God. What am I seeing?*

I then thought about this question for a few seconds, but that was all. I was a carefree child, and I spent most of my time enjoying life and playing all day. I was a shy kid, and I didn't get love from my mother in the right way. I was raised with ignorance, and ignorance is the opposite of love.

It's important to note that I grew up during the civil war of 1997. I was seven years old when I first saw fireworks. In truth, they were bullets falling from the sky like rain. It was beautiful!

That's what I thought at that age, but many people died, and many others were killing each other over two dollars or for other stupid reasons. It was a nightmare, more for adults than kids, for those old enough to know about war and guns.

At that time, everyone in Albania could own a gun, even kids. Toys were more expensive than real guns. We got most of the guns for free. People were afraid. To protect themselves, they kept Kalashnikovs in their homes, shooting into their gardens to scare away intruders. I was seven years old when I first fired a Kalashnikov. My uncle had given it to me, and he was proud of how I handled the weapon. I learned how to use an AK-47 at the same age, and most Albanians will proudly say the same thing. Personally, I never shared their enthusiasm.

One morning, after some shooting, I saw smoke rising from our neighbour's roof. I called my uncle and the others. We went to their house, and I saw my friend Toni holding an AK. We asked what had happened.

Toni said, 'I don't wanna see any ants on my ceiling. I hate those shitty insects.'

Just to kill ants, my crazy friend had shot holes into his ceiling!

At that time, the Kalashnikov was the solution to most of our problems.

The civil war lasted for one year, and many people gave back their guns when the war ended. Some people kept their guns, though, and it was not unusual to hear gunfire in the streets.

My teen years were difficult, and they became more challenging when I lost the only person I ever loved. I was sixteen when I fell in love for the first time. She was a girl in my class, one of the most beautiful girls in the school. She was perfect for me—white skin, green eyes, long hair, and red lips. I loved her so much; I couldn't stop thinking about her. If I couldn't love others, maybe it was because I had saved all my love for her. One day, this sun-like light went away, and darkness replaced it. In truth, we were just friends. I never hugged her or kissed her, but I loved her more than myself.

I felt that I had lost everything—my light, my hope, my energy, even my desire to live. I didn't have any support to help me move on from this ordeal. I didn't want to feel anything! I wanted to deactivate my emotions, if at all possible. I became depressed. An obscure and mysterious energy was born inside me. I started to play with it. This new power consumed my imagination. It was a game which I lost. I became disorientated. I became passive, and I found it difficult to control myself. Because I didn't want to feel anything, I became a robot. My new life philosophy was based on the *Matrix* series, in which robots take over the world. In those movies, the main characters can't separate human beings from robots. I began to disassociate from society, my friends, my lovers, and people in general. I became the insect in *The Metamorphosis.*

The situation became more complicated when my older brother came home from abroad and started to establish his gangster reputation. He was the bad guy, and Albanians like that. One time, he fired two AKs at the same time—fighting, shooting, and bleeding. He became an iconic Albanian bad boy. However, when one person is crowned the best, new challengers will always emerge.

Meanwhile, I was a disordered soul. I suffered from being a prisoner of my own self. The darkness had invaded me. I lost my feelings, lost my ability to see life's colours, and I lost my energy. Isolated in my room most of time, I started to ask myself, *Why I was born? What is my purpose in life? Who created the universe?*

I had fallen into a deep depression, and I considered suicide. No way, though—I had still dreams I wished to pursue. I wanted to go away. Why not France? I had finished my French-language studies, and I hoped to visit the country. It wasn't so easy, though. Albania was not part of the European Union, and France had imposed some strict immigration laws. I had worked for three months just to pay to take a hopeless exam. My father had promised me that he would take care of the rest, but he didn't keep his word. The exam fee was too expensive for him. I lost all hope and desire to pursue my dream.

I spent a lot of time in front of my computer. Fortunately, I discovered another way of leaving my country. I discovered a French site called Chambre Facile, and I found a host offering an exchange. I would work a few hours per day, and my food and accommodations would then be free. It was much easier than other processes. I didn't hesitate to sign up for a premium membership, and I started to write to people all around France. In total, there were only forty such offers throughout the entire country. I wrote to most of them, and the first positive answer I received came from a lady living in a small town called St-Étienne, in central France.

We spoke by phone and exchanged some emails. Legally, I was only allowed to stay for three months in the Schengen area. She looked kind and was ready to risk harbouring someone without papers. The exchange consisted of taking care of her garden and her small cottage, which she rented to tourists. She told me that her friend had a small business, which presented an opportunity for me to find work. I couldn't believe this was happening.

A hazy light started to appear in front of me, but it was still far away and difficult to see.

2

NEW BEGINNING

I arrived at the St-Étienne train station, after taking a bus from Grenoble. It took me two days to travel from the airport in Milan, Italy, to St-Étienne. It was difficult to feel my legs, but I walked along, pulling my big suitcase. I could feel the air of change. It was a new beginning, but the excitement was lost on me. I found a taxi nearby, and I paid ten euros for a ride to my destination.

The taxi driver knew the place. After ten minutes, we stopped in front of two small houses. I got inside the fence, and I saw a beautiful green garden with big trees and flowers. It was a sunny day—a nice, welcoming day. There was a note hanging on the door: 'I'll be back after five—Madeleine.' I went inside, and I saw the living room, a small chimney, and the kitchen. I found two rooms upstairs, one of which was ready for me. I collapsed on the bed. I was so tired, and I still had a three-hour wait.

I fell asleep. Hearing a strange voice, I woke up. I saw an old lady with round glasses, smiling at me. This was Madeleine. I didn't hesitate to give her a hug. I explained what my situation in Albania had been. I had seen a psychologist, and I took some antidepressants.

As I told her about all of this, Madeleine looked me in the eye and said, 'Martin, you have beautiful teeth!'

I knew that I was handsome, and I was lucky that society had accepted me. However, in my kind of situation, it didn't always work well.

After we discussed my life story in detail, Madeleine was a bit disappointed. Regardless, she was kind, and she assured me that I had made the right decision to leave Albania.

The next morning, we went into town. It was a small city, but it was very chic, with a lot of expensive shops. After a nice walk, we stopped at a pizzeria. The pizza cost twenty-five euros. It was all so expensive, and I wasn't even in Paris. Madeleine said that these prices were common in this small town.

I started to work little jobs around the house—cutting trees, cleaning, and arranging some stuff in the cellar.

Madeleine was a good cook, and I already enjoyed French food. Things were going well.

One morning, she called her friend M. Lany. He came over later that day, and we discussed what I was capable of doing and what he could offer. At first, he offered me just two days' work at his house and another day at his parents' house. I did a nice job on his property, and then went to his parents' house. After I finished my work at his parents' house, he paid me in euros and also gave me a gift—a beautiful, brand-new bike.

I was so happy to have met so many helpful, nice people.

Soon afterwards, Madeleine decided to go to the Caribbean for three months. She wanted me to remain in France to take care of her house and her cottage. She was rich, and she often talked to me about her wealthy lifestyle. Her husband had been a smart man, and he did everything he could to earn money. They were rich, but they weren't happy. After I had told her my story, Madeleine told me hers. Her life was horrible. Her husband had committed suicide. He had shot himself in front of their children, and their son had died as the result of a heroin overdose. These stories reminded me that I was not the only one suffering in this mad world.

One day before she left for the Caribbean, I was telling Madeleine about my life philosophy, and she showed me an interesting experiment. She took two crooked iron sticks and moved in front of me. At a distance of metre and half, nothing happened. At one metre away, and I saw the iron sticks begin to slowly move backwards. I took the sticks, and I started to move in front of her. At one metre, nothing happened. Another half a metre away, the iron sticks started to move backwards.

Madeleine explained the phenomenon: 'Do you see the difference, Martin? The iron sticks started to move at a further distance away when I was in front of you. That shows that you have more energy than I do because you are younger and much stronger. We used these sticks a long time ago to find water sources.'

I began to change my idea of being a robot. A simple experiment showed me that we have energy around our bodies, but we don't see it, and it's difficult to feel it.

Alone in the house after Madeleine left for the Caribbean, I thought it would be good to work on my attitude. I soon found the best thing to get rid of my deep depression: the cat I had to care of for Madeleine. This animal became my only friend. I didn't know too much about animals, but I started to learn. Animals have feelings, and cats especially can feel your energy. I understood that when I felt angry, the cat mostly stayed away from me. But when I was calm, if I lay down on the coach, he would just approach and wait for cuddles.

I spent three months alone in Madeleine's house, going outside to ride my bike and walk every day. It was winter, but I didn't mind the cold. When inside the house, I watched TV or played on Madeleine's computer.

After three months away, Madeleine came back. The situation started to change directly. She wasn't the same as before. As soon as she arrived, I saw that she was frustrated. She had an accident in the Caribbean, and she wasn't satisfied with how I was taking care of her house. Even though I did all she asked me to do, I couldn't please her. During the days that followed, she began shouting and screaming. Maybe she needed help, but I wasn't capable of providing it.

I wanted to change my living arrangements. The only choice was a place in Paris, with a French lady who worked for an association in Albania. I had met her during a ceremony at my college; fortunately, I had still her contact information. I explained my situation to her, and she said that I could live with her. Of course, I would have to work in exchange for food and lodging.

Paris! I couldn't believe that I was actually going to Paris—much less that I would live there.

I took the train, traveling for four hours, stopping at Bercy Station, and then taking the metro. The last person I asked took out his smartphone and showed me a map of the street where I was headed. If I had my own GPS, it would be much easier to find addresses without asking. Anyway, speaking fluent French makes me happy, so I can't be lost.

I reached the address and knocked on the door After waiting five minutes at the front door, I finally saw the person I thought would save me. I didn't know that I could be saved by a pony. Soon after, I discovered her donkey brain and her piggy body—completely nude. I now understood the kind of person who was waiting for me.

Her first question was, 'How old are you?'

'Twenty-four,' I answered.

She looked me in the eye and said, 'You are so young!'

Oh yeah. She was waiting for a boyfriend! I never had sex with the girl I loved—or any other girls. I didn't want to start with a fifty-seven-year-old lady.

Nine cats surrounded me when I entered. The tenth cat was the woman herself, a savage dirty old cat. Everywhere I looked, I saw pictures of cats, cat statues, and cat books. She was obsessed with these animals. Sometimes I even saw her talking to them. Her favourite was the oldest one, with a blind eye like a pirate.

The house was situated close to the centre of the city, and I could see the Eiffel Tower when I looked out the windows.

The first week, she was kind because I was working well in the house. I cleaned everything—starting from vacuuming, to emptying the cellar and repairing the cement walls. I continued to work hard as the weeks passed. Was she satisfied? No way! The savage old bitch was never satisfied with my work. The satisfaction she wanted was for me to jump her big old ass. I could sleep with someone older, even sixty years old, but not with this one. Even if I had to spend two months suffering, I was not sleeping with her. She promised to pay me fifteen euros a day for the work I was doing, plus food and lodging. It was a good deal for me, even though I knew that I deserved more.

One week we spent in a village in Bourgogne, in another property she had inherited. I had to help her with packing and selling all the stuff she wanted to get rid of. I worked all day, justifying to myself that I would do everything necessary just to not fuck her, even though we shared the same bed. But she didn't miss the opportunity to get half naked in front of me. If I wasn't afraid of what had happened to me up to now, at that moment, I was afraid. After seeing this pig naked yet again, I ran out of the room. After five minutes, I came back, and I saw an evil human being. Oh yeah, I could see in her eyes how angry she became.

I was pushing the limit by staying in her house, and I started to search for another host on the same site where I had started my adventure. I found someone in Bordeaux. Not an exchange this time. This offered me a cabin for two hundred euros per month. It was still a good deal if I got paid by the cat lady.

Often I had to defend myself during my stay with her, but, when the moment to pay me arrived, she threw three hundred euros at me, saying, 'Defend yourself now!'

The next morning, I paid one hundred euros for a train ticket to Bordeaux, and I had the rest of the money to pay for the cabin. I travelled for hours on that train, and I was the happiest guy. I couldn't believe that I was going to Bordeaux. While in Albania, I dreamed so much about this city. Now I was living the dream, even though I had so little money.

My plan was to find a job soon as possible and earn some money so that I could survive. I knew that it could be hard to find a job without a visa, but I would never stop and would die trying.

I was lucky to be hosted by a yoga teacher called Charlotte. Directly she became my salvation angel. From the beginning I was honest about my situation, and she was very kind to accept someone who needed help. She proposed an exchange of working a few hours on her garden and getting food for free. I was lucky!

The village was called Cadillac. I could see vineyards and wine castles everywhere. I hoped to find some work there, but it was April, and harvesting started in September.

We arrived at Charlotte's house. To the left was the cabin where I would stay for a month. There was a comfortable bed, but I only stayed in the cabin at night, to sleep, and shared the house with Charlotte during the day.

Next door there was a big room for yoga practise. I was curious to know more about this art, and I asked Charlotte for help. She suggested that I read some books so I could learn about yoga after practising. It's not only gymnastic; you also have to meditate, relax, listen to your body, and learn to softly extend your muscles.

I was surrounded by beautiful nature, and I often walked outside. I could feel the pure fresh air of France, and I couldn't stop walking for hours, feeding myself with this green energy. Soon after arriving in Bordeaux, I started to feel the first changes in my body from yoga, a new way of thinking and moving. I started to believe that there was a cure for my problems, and it was there in nature—for free.

I went to the local mission to ask for a job. I had no papers. I had already passed my limited time in the Schengen area, but I didn't want to stay passive, doing nothing. At this time of crisis, there was no hope of tolerance. It was difficult for those in France legally to find work; for those there illegally, it was almost impossible. Any public employment agency respected the country's laws 100 per cent. There was definitely no solution in regard to getting a job this way.

I didn't care too much that I didn't have money; I was enjoying my stay with Charlotte. I had good food and good company. Charlotte suggested some other books for me to read. She gave a book called *The Alchemist,* by Paulo Coelho, telling me that it could be interesting for me to read a story of a guy who travelled to find his destiny. That book stayed on my bed for two weeks, but I didn't read it.

I started to read another book, called *The Pacific Warrior.* I learned a lot of things in this book, which talks about an imaginary master, vegetarianism, happiness, and acrobatics. An interesting piece of advice includes how to maintain our bodies in perfect shape. How to be happy was a good advice for me also, but could I do it? I had forgotten how to be happy. I read an interesting story of this master, describing ancient peoples who walked the earth and searched for ways to survive. The darkness came, and they had to find a place to stay. They found a cavern and went into it. They closed the cavern with a stone, but it was too dark inside. So, they discovered fire. The artificial light began shining on their souls. After they saw their shadows on the walls, they started to play with them. They were so happy passing a good time in front of the fire and playing. But some of the people got bored, so they decided to push the stone away and search for the real light.

I compared myself with the people who went away to search for the sun. I went away from Albania, which I could call a cavern. For me, the fire represents material things; it is an artificial light symbolic of money, cars, and everything expensive.

The days passed quickly, and I began losing hope of finding work. I searched everywhere in the region, asking people for any kind of work. As always, there were no positive answers for those there illegally. I started to search the Internet, looking for different jobs, including volunteer jobs, and I discovered a site called Volunteer Help. It was a miracle to find that site at the moment I had begun to lose hope of surviving. I was almost done at Charlotte's house, and I had to find contacts on Volunteer Help. The cost of using the site was twenty euros for two years. Charlotte who paid for it, and she did it with pleasure, knowing my situation. I began to write to many contacts, so I could get as many answers as possible.

I could write to a maximum of twenty people closest to where I was in Bordeaux. From all these requests, I got six positive answers, at different times. The first came from a couple just forty-five kilometres away, in Dordogne, a department in western France. After spending time there, Dordogne became my favourite region in France.

It was kind of Charlotte to bring me straight to the place, her last favour to me. I never forgot all she did for me. I started to walk in a quiet neighbourhood with nice houses and big gardens. I saw people working in the gardens, and I didn't hesitate to ask for Arthur and Ines. One of the people I asked told me that it was easy; just to follow the road, and the last house on the left was their property.

Just before I arrived, I noticed a creepy lady staring at me. She was in the middle of the road, and I asked her about the address, just to make sure I was in the right place.

'Are you really going there? Do you know them?' she asked.

'No,' I said, a bit worried by the way she said the words.

'Do not go there; they are strange people! How did you get here?' the creepy lady asked.

'Someone brought me here, but she just left. What's wrong with them? Can you tell me? Can you explain it to me?' My voice rose because I was really worried now.

'Just go, and you will see,' she said, and then she walked on.

Five minutes later, I was at the front door, knocking. Ines opened the door and smiled at me. Then, I saw Arthur. Very kindly he showed me each part of the house and, of course, my room. I couldn't believe I had found such a nice room made ready for me. Imagine going from a cabin to a place like this, sleeping somewhere else with people you didn't know but who treated you with such kindness when welcoming you. I understood that my dream had just started.

We would wake up at seven o'clock in the morning, eating breakfast with butter and jam, milk and chocolate. We then started work at eight o'clock.

The first day, Arthur showed me his new plan for the garden. We had to build a fence for the chickens, digging a trench and putting up a metal net. First, I started to dig the holes for the posts that would hold the net. Arthur looked a bit tired, because of his age, and I asked him if I could do the work on my own. When the bell rang, he asked me to leave the tools and sit with him for lunch. Each working day, when the bell rang, it was a signal of midday, the time to finish work. The meals were delicious, prepared by Ines with love and care.

I was happy with them, and yet, at the same time, I knew that I could only stay for two weeks. One thing I enjoyed a lot was walking along the Dordogne river, the purest of all the rivers in France. Walking and meditating, leaving my past behind, listening to Lindsey Stirling, and sometimes even running, getting that unlimited green energy. I never grew tired of walking. Nature became my therapy, and Dordogne was the best therapist. Suddenly I had a vision of building my house on the border of this magical river. Even dreams can be kind of energy; all positive thoughts and visions are the same, helping us to go forward, believe in ourselves, and know that nothing is impossible.

I learned a lot from Arthur. He was a professional woodworker. I learned how to build a fence and a small cabin. Once a week, we went to take care of his hives. It was my first time working with bees, and I learned how to do the transvasion and disinfection. He produced the honey himself with a small machine in his garage, putting stamps on the pots and selling the honey to neighbours and a few people around the village. I think it was a nice way for him to occupy himself. He told me that he owned many apartments, which he rented, but he still had to work hard to make a normal life. Work keeps your life in balance, even if you are a billionaire.

The second response from Volunteer Help was from a sixty-one-year-old lady called Grace, living just fifty kilometres away. I called her, and she explained what the work in her house was like: cutting the grass, planting, painting, and putting a new plinth on a garden column. I didn't know how to do the last one, but I didn't say anything.

My last day with Arthur and Ines was sad for me. They gave me some pocket money and two pots: one with jam and the other with honey. I gave them each a hug and got ready for my next destination.

I waited just a few minutes in the train station, and Grace picked me up with her small Renault Twingo. She could speak a few languages, including Italian, and we started talking to each other in this language.

We soon arrived in a green and cosy village called Bouillac, still in the department of Dordogne.

Grace's house was small and had a pointy roof. After opening the door, I could see crystals everywhere, and I was curious about them.

'Why so many crystals, Grace? I know they look nice in the house, but there is another reason, isn't there?

'Crystals have energy, Martin,' Grace explained.

I learned more about energy from Grace, in an exaggerated way, it seemed to me. She called herself a healer, and she was part of a sect believing in energy which came from the universe.

The first few days, I worked in the garden. Afterwards, I started with the plinth, which I didn't find difficult, even my first time.

Her cooking was simple, but tasty after a day's work of course. Originally from Britain, she spent most of her time with her family in Copenhagen. I tried different dishes she made, but I often forgot to say that it was good or offer any kind of compliment to satisfy her. After trying a delicious soup with chicken and rice, I noticed she looked a bit upset. I enjoyed the meal, and that was all; I forgot to pay her a compliment for her cooking.

'Martin! In Copenhagen, every day, after each meal, we say, "*Takk for maten!*" Which means, "Thank you for the meal!".'

'Sorry, Grace. It was delicious; I mean, I loved it. Thank you so much.' My voice was more powerful than ever.

It was a sunny day, and she decided to wake me for a tour around the region. We drove for half an hour along the Dordogne river. Behind a mountain plateau appeared the most beautiful village I have ever seen. Called Beynac, it had a big castle on top of the hill and some old stone houses covering the hillsides. The river, the houses, and the castle on top—it was fascinating.

It was May, and the area was filled with tourists visiting this magical part of Dordogne, some walking and others sailing on boats on the river. We walked all the way up to the castle, relaxing in a restaurant where I tried a sweet wine accompanied by cake.

Often I would think to myself, *I don't know how I will finish up here, or where I'll be next week, but I'm happy … happy!*

It was a good day tour, and the sun kept shining till the evening.

The next day, I was ready for work.

I was cutting grass in the garden, and Grace was picking some vegetables to use for cooking.

She passed nearby, and she screamed, 'Don't move!'

I didn't move, of course, after hearing her scream.

'Stop! Don't move, Martin! Look behind you; there's a flower behind you. Be careful! Do not touch it.'

I saw a yellow flower, and I didn't dare to move even a centimetre.

She approached and carefully touched the flower.

'Flowers have energy, Martin. Everything alive has energy, has life.'

'But, Grace, you are walking on the grass now, which I just cut.'

This theory that everything's alive can make us a bit contradictory. I respect nature, but if I saw a pretty girl, I wouldn't hesitate to cut a flower and give to her. No one alive can judge my gesture, which express the purest energy: love.

I told Grace that my solution for healing myself could happen by falling in love with a girl.

To this, she replied directly, 'First, you have to love yourself, young man!'

Taking Grace's advice was hard. After hearing all her stories, I always felt good, and she said that it was her giving me energy. But, when we spoke about choices, it was me choosing this life, my parents, before I was born. It was a deep philosophy that I couldn't accept if I wanted to change myself in the easiest way possible.

We started talking about ghosts in the house, people who had lived there before. Late one afternoon, I saw a pretty girl with long hair, wearing a pink T-shirt, pass in front of the house. I could clearly see her nice figure, and I had some red visions for a few seconds.

I then came back inside the house, going to bed after a long day's work. My room was small, with a comfortable bed and a big window. I watched the stars' reflection cast on the ceiling through the window at night. It was a nice view before closing my eyes.

I saw a ghost approach to me. It wore a pink T-shirt and had no face. He came and started to push me from my bed. I was afraid! I was dreaming. I woke up, but in the dream! This feeling made my dream a bit special. I woke up and saw the stars through the window. I was looking at the universe.

I thought, *I'm watching the stars now; I'm watching the universe. I don't have to be afraid. This is just a dream.*

I slept again. In the dream this ghost always came and started to push me again.

This time, I was really afraid, and I decided to go to Grace's room, even though I didn't want to show my fear in front of her.

'Grace, there's a ghost in my room, and I'm afraid. It's a guy without face, wearing a pink T-shirt.'

'Don't be afraid, Martin! I know him. He's a kind person.'

I came back to my room, and the ghost appeared again and started doing the same thing. I wasn't afraid any more. I knew he was kind; maybe he wanted just to play with me. After he pushed me, I pushed him back, and we kept doing this. We were playing with each other. I became friends with the ghost.

I woke up in the morning, quickly going downstairs, and started to tell Grace about my dream.

After hearing about the pink T-shirt, she said, 'Pink! Pink is love. This colour always represents love, and it signifies love in your dream.'

Love! It was a boy wearing it. Why a boy? Why not a girl! I thought briefly, but I soon started to understand the sense of this special dream which would follow me throughout my journey. If I wanted to restart everything in another way, to give a sense to my life, I had to believe even in dreams. Some might be messages, arrows showing us the path to the truth.

I started talking to Grace about my journey and how I was learning and improving myself along the way.

She suggested that I read *The Alchemist* by Paulo Coelho, which was the same book that Charlotte had given me.

'Martin, you have to read this book!' Grace said. 'It's about a guy who travels, just like you.'

'Well, if it's the same thing I'm doing, no thanks; I don't wanna read my own story,' I replied.

But she had already ordered the book via the Internet. It arrived by post the day I was leaving.

I thought, *I really should read this book!*

Grace paid for the book and also gave me a gift: a pink crystal. She provided some pocket money as well for the nice job I had done.

The next adventure brought me to a castle, a wine factory near the famous St-Émilion. A British couple would host me this time, the first Brits to accept my invitation since I'd started my journey. I had arranged in advance to stay for a maximum of three weeks, but I actually didn't stay even a week. I had good company from people coming from different countries: two guys from New Zealand, one girl from Germany, one from China, and another from Belgium. An American came the day before I left. Working the grapes was hard. It was hot, and I had to work longer hours than expected: no fewer than seven hours per day. The rules of Volunteer Help offer an exchange of four to five hours of work, five days a week. I was satisfied with the food and drinks. It was my first time trying a wine of 1985 and '90. It is true what they say about old wines: they taste better! Of course, they are much more expensive, but in exchange programs everything they give you is free.

Working in the sun gave me the desire to find another opportunity near the coast. I wanted to see the sea, so I started to write to people living along the southern coast of France. The first positive answer came from Antoine, who lived just outside Arles, in a village called Mont-Major Abbey.

After six days at the winery, I took the train from Bordeaux straight to Arles. It was a long trip, and I passed the time reading *The Alchemist,* a book which I really enjoyed. At first, it looked like other books I had read, but I found some interesting passages, which I believed had led me to read it.

Here is the first such passage: 'At a certain point in our lives, we lose control of what's happening to us, and our lives become controlled by fate. That's the world's greatest lie.'

Of course, I had to agree with that. I felt lost but not losing control of myself. I knew there were choices I could make chances I could take, all of which would determine my destiny.

Here is the second interesting passage: 'When you really want something in your life, all the universe conspires in helping you to achieve it.'

That sounded so unreal, and yet the universe was big and magical, and so I believed that what I read must be true.

After a five-hour train trip, I got at the Arles train station. Antoine was waiting in front of the parking. A tall man with white hair, wearing headphones. I understood directly his casual way of meeting people, which I liked.

'Where is your car?' I asked him, pulling my suitcase behind me.

'I didn't come by car Martin. We'll pick up the bus,' he said.

We were walking on the sidewalk by the sea, where I saw a bridge.

At the same time, Antoine grabbed a photo from a Chinese girl selling souvenirs on the street. He showed the photo to me, saying, 'The bridge you see in front of you is Langlois Bridge. It is in some of the most famous Van Gogh paintings.

Antoine's house was twenty-five minutes away. We got off the bus, walked along, and stopped in front of a white door. Above the door was a wooden plank that read, 'Van Gogh was never here and never lived here!' The building was in the *chambre d'hôtes* old style, with stones. The interior was decorated in a sophisticated way. On the first floor there was a small bar, with two verandas outside. Antoine showed me all the rooms. My favourite was the Van Gogh room. It was perfect, with each detail copied from original Van Gogh masterpieces. This was why Antoine had to put a sign on the front door to tell tourists that his house was not a museum.

After my tour of the house, Antoine asked me if I wanted to join him for a trip to the beach. What kind of question was that for someone who had come just for the sea? I was so excited! I expressed my desire, and suddenly it just happened. It had to be magic, right?!

Antoine was magical too. I understood this from my first day there, and I didn't hesitate to tell him my whole story. Of course, he understood me. After hearing all I said, he suggested that I not tell everyone because a sad story made people sad as well.

We went to meet his friends, wherein I had to work not more than nine days. The job consisted only of painting the interior of an old apartment.

The first evening, I enjoyed eating dinner with a lot of people around.

Antoine's best friend, called Mark, was very polite, but his girlfriend was not.

The first time we met she asked me, 'Erm, Martin, you are Muslim, right? What do people in your country think about gay people?'

Without hesitating a second, I answered, 'A gay man in Albania is a dead man!'

I said the truth, but I didn't know the truth of the situation in group of friends. Antoine was gay, but I couldn't distinguish it in any detail about him.

After finishing my work in the apartment the first day, I went to Antoine's house. He told me the story between Antoine, Mark, and his girlfriend. She was jealous because Mark spent a lot of time with Antoine, and people started to talk about them, saying that Antoine was Mark's lover. Not only was she jealous, she was also ashamed.

I don't like gay people. For me, their lifestyle goes against nature, and I respect the laws of nature. I could make an exception with Antoine, after getting to know him, and consider him as a friend. He had suffered early on in his life, and apart from being gay, he had a strong character, was very smart, and seemed to be a key player in his society.

I told Antoine that I was happy in Albania just playing a game, an online ship game called Seafight, on an Italian server. I played five hours a day for an entire year. It was my drug, in which I lost myself in the most pleasurable moments. The beautiful part of that game was that I could speak at the same time as I was playing. Speaking every day, it became difficult even for the Italians to distinguish me from themselves.

'Do you want to be happy, Martin? You have to play again, but this time in real life. That's what I do to be on top of the rest,' said Antoine.

On that game I was called Joker, so I had to the same in ordinary life as well. This name could be the key to happiness for people who have lost their ability to feel. To play with people's lives?! Maybe, but I didn't want to hurt anyone for no reason, just to play and lie about my true self.

When I told Antoine that I wanted to fall in love with a girl to heal myself, his answer was 'Try first to love yourself!'

I hadn't believed Grace when she gave me the same advice, but I wanted to believe Antoine because he was more intelligent and his advice was more concrete. I started to think about my dream with the ghost wearing the pink T-shirt that Grace had said was the colour of love. Maybe that guy was me! Maybe it was a message to love myself.

Antoine suggested another site, Work Exchange, for me to contact hosts. He said it was the same as Volunteer Help but even easier. Travelling was my means of survival, and I didn't hesitate for a second to give him thirty euros to open a new account.

I had to work only five hours a day and spent the rest of my time walking around the village. On my day off, I took the bus to Arles, a small town filled with culture and art which was unfolded everywhere—on buildings, in the streets, in people's clothes, and in the whole lifestyle.

I enjoyed my stay in Arles for one week only. I then had to write to someone else nearby. When I finished the work in Arles, I felt that I had to move, even though Mark said that I could stay longer if I wanted. I emailed five hosts, copying and pasting the same text, and then I waited for the replies. The first positive response was from a Flemish couple living in the same region, around 180 kilometres away, in a small town called Divajeu. They owned a castle B & B. I didn't check the details in their profile; their answer was enough for me. I was excited to start a new adventure.

I didn't have much money left, so Antoine suggested that I hitch-hike to the next destination. He'd already made some signs with the names of cities I would have to pass through.

I met with Antoine and his friends for the last time and then went straight to the road. Lifting my right hand, with my thumb up, I waited. This was the first time I tried this kind of trip, which I now call a lucky way of travelling. I had to wait just three minutes for a car to stop in front of me. Extending his hand from the window, he waved to me to get in, and I threw my suitcase in the back seat and got in beside him in the front.

It was a one-hour trip to Nîmes. I knew I was lucky, since I only had to wait just a few minutes before someone picked me up without knowing me at all, ready to offer a trip for free just in exchange for conversation. Life is so easy, and yet, most of the time, we don't have the courage to see that it is as easy as it is.

The second time, I wasn't as lucky as the first. I had to wait forty minutes. Most drivers don't care about hitch-hikers, maybe because they have never tried to travel this way. Some are afraid of unknown people, some are late on their own journeys, and the rest just do not want to bother with those who have lost their way.

After forty minutes of waiting, I saw a Mercedes slow to a stop. The driver was shirtless, so I only half lifted my finger; I wasn't sure about this one. Suddenly he stopped and got out of the car. He grabbed my suitcase and put it in his car. He was around twenty years old, a mulatto from Morocco. I started to tell him my story. After he paid the toll, he gave me ten euros in coins. It was more than I expected from someone who offered me a trip for free.

The next one was an old man in a new BMW. This was a comfortable trip as well. After I introduced myself, he offered me his phone so that I could call my family in Albania. I declined. Next, he offered to stop at the nearest McDonald's. Everything was free in hitch-hiking, without any exchange; just free travel and free offers.

I got out of the BMW when we stopped in a town called Bollene, and another driver picked me up. We travelled a short distance, and he gave me some croissants and a bottle of water when we parted. The next driver was a young woman, a French teacher. The one after her was also a French teacher, but she worked in Iceland. The last was a retired couple who brought me straight to the castle called Chateau Legrand, my destination.

To make sure it was the right one, I asked a lady passing nearby.

'Yes,' she answered, curious as she looked at me.

I started to tell her about my travels via the Work Exchange site.

Strangely enough, her face changed, and she asked, 'Who brought you here? Do you know the people you are going to?'

'I came by hitch-hiking, but thank you for the confirmation; that's all I need to know.'

This was the second time I'd had this answer, and I hoped for the same result as the last time.

I stood in front of a huge stone castle. I then went inside, following the stairs up to the veranda, where I saw a big, fat man with a moustache, waiting for me.

'Welcome to the chateau, Martin! I was waiting for you.'

'I finally found you, Noah! Thanks for the welcome.'

He offered me a beer, and we started to talk. He's wife came a bit later. A big, blonde, fat lady, with a pretty face and blue eyes, called Isabella.

'Martin, we are so happy to have you here! You know, after those comments in our profile, it was difficult for us to get more volunteers.'

I didn't read their comments, so I wouldn't be surprised to learn something strange about them, especially after meeting their neighbour.

To talk with Noah was like reading an encyclopaedia. What I remember most was the end of that discussion, when he mentioned something about world government.

In reply I said, 'Maybe aliens are on top of that!'

And they looked strangely each other.

I was joking but, as we say in Albania, sometimes jokes are half of the truth. With Noah and Isabella, I soon discovered that my joke was 100 per cent their truth.

I expected to have a nice room in the castle, but Noah sent me to a cabin two hundred metres away, in the woods. At least I found a neatly arranged space and a comfortable bed. Outside I found a convertible shower and dry toilets. I didn't mind this. During my adventure, I accepted any kind of risk, and to take a shower in the made my adventure unique.

The next morning, I visited the castle. There was a nice pool, with an amazing view of a nearby mountain and eagles flying around it.

The first day, I did only outside cleaning, but in the days that followed, I started to switch to the normal routine. I would wake up at eight o'clock in the morning, clean the pool, clean the rooms, and change the bed sheets. I did a lot of work outside the castle as well, mostly cutting the grass, which was two metres high in places. I joined them only for lunch. For the rest of my meals, they gave me some cheap boxes of prepared food which you could get at the supermarket for two euros each. Whatever. Seeing the work I did all day long, they offered to pay me fifty euros per week.

I had to go to the nearest supermarket, five kilometres away, to buy what I wanted. I then discovered Nutella, with which I fell in love at first taste. I couldn't stop eating it, which I justified to myself by reasoning that I didn't have anything else better to eat. I could walk ten kilometres just to buy a 450-gram jar of Nutella. I ate it with my finger during the walk back to the cabin, and by the time I got there, I had finished half of it; so, I had to go to the same shop the next week to buy another jar.

It was interesting to talk with Noah, to discover his vast and creepy knowledge.

One day, I wore a black shirt with some white messy drawings printed on it.

Noah looked at it and said, 'Martin, what are those designs on your shirt?'

'Picasso-style drawings,' I answered.

The next day, I wore the same shirt, and Noah became even more agitated, saying, 'Martin! Don't wear that shirt any more!'

Late in the afternoon that same day, Noah started talking about aliens, telling me that he had received signs from them ever since he was a youth. He also told me that he could see them in the pool's reflections, sometimes for as long as two whole days.

He had schizophrenia! Yes, I had to accept that he was mentally ill, but I couldn't deny his knowledge or wisdom. He read a lot of books, and any time I mentioned a theory, he could connect it with the appropriate philosopher.

I asked him for some general theories about life, especially my life.

He started to explain, asking my horoscope sign.

When I told him, he said, 'Yes, you are a fish. I noticed that by the way you're traveling, sliding into countries.'

'Do you think really that I chose my parents, Noah?'

'Yes, Martin, you chose them! But don't forget that after we make a choice, we become slaves of this world. We are slaves.'

'Slaves?! Look at you. You are rich, you have a big castle, good people around, a beautiful wife—just think about the present,' I said. 'Do you believe in Eckhart Tolle's theories?'

'Sorry, but I don't have any idea what that is.'

'Eckhart Tolle's theories explain that we have to think about and enjoy our present to keep ourselves in harmony.'

'But that's wrong because the past is tightly connected to us,' he argued.

'Well, what do you mean about us being slaves?'

'I can give you an example, starting with the biggest head in the world, Obama. He's a marionette. There are some people very powerful on top of the world. They are our real governance, and we don't have any idea who they are, what they look like, or where they come from.'

I was attracted by his knowledge and wanted to ask Noah to give me ideas about how to earn money.

'How can I make money?' I asked.

'You can start with gold, Martin. The price of gold price is going up. You can start in your country, buying small things like rings, necklaces, or bracelets, and then sell them in Italy at a higher price.'

After I told him about Kalashnikovs in Albania, he offered me another idea.

'I need a Kalashnikov, Martin,' he said. 'I have two more friends who need guns as well. Start with that and then expand your business. You can get a new Kalashnikov here for three thousand euros, but I know in your country you can easily find it for five hundred or less.'

What he said was true, but I didn't want to start earning money by going into the gun business. At the moment, money meant nothing to me. I was searching for something more precious than anything I could buy. I wanted more than material things, more even than positive feelings; I wanted the real, pure thing that mattered: love.

It was July, and a lot of tourists were coming. I had really good contacts with them, not only serving but also playing and having nice conversations. A family from the Netherlands—a beautiful mother and daughter, and a generous father—became special friends. I had really good time with them, and before they left, they invited me to visit their house in Amsterdam. I didn't think too much about visiting the Netherlands, considering my illegal status.

I didn't enjoy my last days in the castle. Isabella changed her attitude towards me. I started to write emails to other hosts in the area. No answer. All were occupied during the summer. I wrote again, via Work Exchange, and the first positive answer came from a village called Oiac, 350 kilometres away, in Carcassone. A retired man called Gaspard offered minimal conditions in exchange for building works.

I thought about where I could go for my next adventure, but I felt lost. I wanted to be with people I already knew. Why not write to Arthur and Ines? I had been happy there. I wrote them an email explaining my current situation, but I would have to wait to hear from them.

To go in the medieval city wasn't easy. I had money just to pay for half the trip by carpooling via BlaBlaCar, and I had to hitch-hike the rest of the way. I arrived in the city centre in the late afternoon, where I took the bus. The bus stopped in another village, but Oiac was still far away. I was lost, and I tried to call the host. No answer, so I started to ask people about Oiac village. I was lost, and the village was also.

Someone showed me which way to hitch-hike to get there. Lifting my hand, I stepped into the road and waited. Someone stopped his van, and I asked for a map. Fortunately, he knew the way and suggested where I could hitch-hike again once he dropped me off.

After he left, I found myself in the middle of nowhere, in the dark. I stayed near the road, hoping for late-night drivers. A small black car approached, and I saw an old lady behind the steering wheel. I lifted my hand up, and she stopped a few centimetres away.

'Get in, young man! I don't wanna leave someone in the dark at this hour,' she said.

I was happy because this kind lady was ready to bring me straight to the house, as she knew the host I was going to. In a few minutes, we arrived at the house. We knocked on the door, and Gaspard came out. After a big thank-you to this lady, I entered in the house.

It was an old kitchen, with one other separate room and a bathroom in the same style. We directly sat down and watched the movie *The Fifth Element*. It was an old one, of course, but one of my favourites. After the movie, Gaspard brought me outside and showed me a tent behind the house, where I was to sleep.

It was a beautiful night with stars filling the sky. I went into the small tent, finding two sheets inside but no pillow. It was like sleeping on rocks. At least I had a comfortable bed in the cabin.

During my trip, I learned that when you change to find a better place, it can often be worse. Keep calm, and just respect the general rule of surviving: adapt!

I woke up in the morning, tired from the poor night's sleep. I opened the tent, and the sun was shining. I walked toward the house and saw Gaspard on the veranda. Breakfast was already made. Simple things like butter and jam, some chocolate, but no Nutella. (Some French people don't like Nutella. They consider it unhealthy because it contains palm oil, and so they choose another product which is less expensive. In truth, it's just a justification for the price. All chocolate contains oil from palms or something else; it's all the same.)

Gaspard showed me the work: cutting the wall with a metal saw. Quite hard to start this beautiful day, but I wasn't worried at all; I could accept any kind of work without hesitating. I worked for two hours, rested for fifteen minutes, and started again. I finished the work and, after eating lunch, I had the rest of the day to visit some particular places that Gaspard suggested me. One was a waterfall, just four hundred metres into the woods. Before going there, I couldn't miss visiting the ruined castle near the house. I was surprised that this *hameau* (French for 'small village') had just thirty-nine habitants. As Gaspard explained to me, this area was the least densely populated in all of Europe. I went through the forest, searching for the waterfall along the river, and I found it. What I saw was a pond with water dripping from an altitude of no more than 2 metres. A bit disappointed, I still wouldn't have missed the opportunity to enjoy walking in this wild and beautiful setting.

The work started to get easier when new helpers arrived: a couple from Australia. He was called William, around forty years old, and she was called Lydia, a pretty girl from Germany, not more than twenty years old.

I was still cutting the wall when William came and wanted to grab the saw. He was a builder and a host himself in Melbourne. After eating lunch, we started to talk about travelling, and I was happy to share my story.

When I finished, his eyes were shining, and he asked me, 'Do you like the ocean?'

He was ready to offer me a chance to go to Australia, where he lived, but I didn't want to go that far. I was aware of the strict conditions that this country had in place to discourage immigrants.

'I like when you talk about yourself, Martin,' William said. 'You are like an Australian; you speak with heart. Do not hesitate to tell your story to a girl.'

That girl wasn't far away—a math teacher from Paris, called Jacqueline, twenty-eight years old and ready to meet me! She explained to me that she was helping at Arthur's house for a few weeks. I could only imagine the nice things Arthur and Ines would tell her about me, which surely must be the reason why she wanted to meet me.

Just a day before Jacqueline arrived, Gaspard told William, Lydia, and me where we could find a real waterfall. William had a car, and the site was a fifteen-minute drive away. We got there and started to look around the forest, along the river, when we just heard the sound of water flowing like a rain shower. This was a real waterfall, not like that little pond. We dove into the waterfall and enjoyed the cold water that flowed from it.

The next day, I met Jacqueline. Rarely had I ever felt so appreciated. she was a cute, skinny blonde, taller than me. After I offered her a drink inside the house, we started a conversation, and she explained the reason for her visit. A student in her class talked about Albania, creating a dramatic story and justifying his bad behaviour because of his past in his homeland. She wanted to hear about Albania from another native. She didn't have time to stay longer than to hear my description of my experiences back home, but before she left, I suggested that we go to the waterfall. I just wanted her to see it; I wasn't thinking about romantic gestures—we hardly knew each other long enough for that, and my experience with girls was too limited. I just gave her a hug and felt grateful for her visit.

I enjoyed my time in the good company of William and Lydia. We drove around and discovered the area, including some natural pools along the river filled with tourists. Swimming there during the warm days in August was like living in paradise. While we were driving, I saw a sign for the village Bugarach. I remembered the name of this village from hearing about the Mayan calendar and the apocalypse. it was just five-kilometre drive. The mountain there supposedly became mystical on occasion. I considered the whole story of the Mayan calendar and the apocalypse a big lie which transformed this village into a tourist attraction.

Unfortunately, the couple's stay was short because Lydia had to renew her visa to go back to

Australia. With William's help, though, we finished the work on the second floor, and Gaspard was very satisfied with the result.

After William and Lydia left, I started planning my trip back to Dordogne. I was so happy just thinking about this. I found someone to carpool with till Toulouse, and afterwards I would hitch-hike to Bordeaux.

Just a few days before I left, two American girls came to replace William, Lydia, and me. They told me their story, which gave me the courage to continue mine. They left their country because it was boring for them to work part time, earn just six hundred dollars per month, and have to live with their parents. They wanted a more meaningful life. Their situation was the same as mine. Americans have permission to stay in Europe for no longer than three months, and they had already been to Georgia, Greece, and Spain. They kept searching for work, looking for a better life without caring too much and just enjoying the adventure. They reminded me that it's better to just continue on than to go back to where you began and leave it.

I left Gaspard's house and the travelled the same way that I had arrived: hitch-hiking. A German couple who had just finished their holidays picked me up on their way home. It was 16 August, and people normally finish their holidays during this time.

From Carcassone, it wasn't difficult to hitch-hike to Bordeaux. The longest part of the journey I spent in the good company of a young couple from Grenoble on their way to Bordeaux to buy wine. They were excited about their wedding preparations, eager to satisfy their guests. Why not get the best French wine, in St-Émilion?

The last one to pick me up brought me to the train station of Castillon la Bataille. This small town took its name from the battle when the French defeated the British once and for all in the fifteenth century.

I waited at the train station for Arthur, as he had suggested in our emails. I was happy that I was going back to stay with Arthur and Ines, to walk again along the Dordogne river. I could feel this positive energy in my heart, but then a wind came and suddenly took it away. Yes, I had come back to where I wanted to be, but then what? Would be this be a definitive solution?

Arthur and Ines both came to the train station, and I felt that I was back home, in the place where I wanted to create my future. I still dreamed about building my house in the department of Dordogne and transforming my home into B & B for tourists. I often dreamed only to feel positive energy, which then gave me hope to go forward in a positive way.

At my hosts' home, I went into the kitchen and saw dinner already prepared: a big plate of chicken and rice. When I went in my room, I saw chocolates on the table. These were the first reasons for me to feel happy that I had come back here.

The next morning, I returned to the same routine as during my first stay: wake up at seven o'clock, eat breakfast, and go to work in the garden. Arthur and I started to build the gate on the left side of the fence we'd already made. After that, we began building a cabin to use as dry toilets. When the bell rang, we left our tools and went to sit on the veranda for lunch.

During the afternoon, the sun was shining, and we went to visit the hives for a few hours.

When we finished work, I had some free time to take a walk along the river—the walks which I had missed so much.

In the days that followed, Arthur and I started to discuss my situation. Arthur suggested that it would be better for me to meet with a lawyer than to seek help from a hopeless immigration association. He wanted to give me the chance to become his employee, to create the necessary documents—but without a salary, of course, since he didn't actually need an employee to help him with his hives. His position as the owner of a small business would allow him to help me with the procedures.

We called the nearest lawyer in Bordeaux. She was a lady who looked to be around fifty years old.

Arthur spoke first, explaining my situation to her.

I didn't receive the answers I had hoped to hear.

'You are here illegally, young man,' she said. 'If you want to start the procedure for a visa, you have to go back to your country and receive permission from the French embassy in Albania. Meanwhile, Arthur will have to complete the other procedures of creating a work contract which you will have to show to the embassy. And that's not all. He will also have to post an ad for the job on the biggest French employment site, Pole Emploie. If no French citizen responds to his job posting, he will then be allowed to have someone like you as an employee. Finally, he will have to appear before the commune officials to justify the reason why he wants to hire an Albanian, not a French citizen. Hiring illegals has caused the economic crisis which is still growing in France, right to this very day.'

'How long will the process take?' I asked with little hope.

'At least three months,' answered the lawyer.

This answer was the worst part of the conversation. I simply couldn't accept it! I didn't want to go back to my country and stay there, hopeless, for three months. No way.

After twenty minutes, the lawyer informed us that we owed her eighty-five euros.

Arthur took a hundred euros from his wallet and left the rest.

What surprised me more was the look on his face. He seemed happy to hear what the lawyer had said. Maybe he thought it would be easier to get me to work for him now. I understood the reason as we talked on our way back to the house.

'You know, Martin, I'll spend a lot of time on your procedure, but you have to know that you will not earn a salary from me.'

'I don't need money from you, Arthur. If I can get the visa, I can easily find work somewhere else. I would be very grateful if you help me get the documents.'

After arriving at the house, Martin started to talk to Ines about my situation.

'Now I have to appear before the commune officials and ask permission; I have to park the car there and pay for it. I have to open an account on Pole Emploie as well and do a lot of other things that I don't even actually know yet. All these papers. This is ridiculous!'

'Take it easy, Arthur,' Ines said. 'Dear, tomorrow you go to the commune, and another day you'll get to the next step. One step at a time. We want to help Martin; we are his only hope.'

'Yes, I know,' Arthur said. 'We have to do whatever is possible.'

Ines then came close to me and said, 'Martin, dear, no worries; everything will be fine if you follow the right procedures. We're gonna pay for your ticket to go back to Albania. You worked hard here, and this is something that you deserve.'

The next day, after finishing some work in the garden, we went to the commune office.

The answer was 'We are sorry that we cannot help with this one. You have to go to the prefecture, but not today, because it's closed.'

After waiting half an hour, this was an answer I didn't want to hear.

I asked Arthur if I could become his employee before going back to my country:

'What? What the hell are you thinking? Are you thinking about illegal procedures, maybe?'

'No, I didn't mean that, Arthur.'

'Stop talking, Martin! I'm spending all this time going around for you, and you suggest illegal ways of creating your papers, for me to risk my life for you. You know, I could go to prison if they discovered it. I'm already taking a risk by having someone illegal in my house!'

I understood that I couldn't find the solution with Arthur, even though I had to admit that all he said was true. I had to be fast and search for another host. I began with Work Exchange, and I started to write to those on the list updates. The first email was to a host with a castle B & B in Normandy, called Chateau de Lumière. The description was fascinating. Even the famous French writer Maupassant wrote something about it in his masterpieces. The work consisted of serving and preparing breakfast for tourists, along with some painting and gardening. It was perfect; the kind of job I enjoyed most. A few hours later, I got the answer I needed, so it wasn't necessary for me to write to anyone else. I left my phone number, and the owner of the castle, Raphael, sent me a message with his address.

It was time to say goodbye to Arthur and Ines, but I didn't to do that—not even a handshake. I had to walk to the train station because they didn't accompany me. It was the coldest goodbye I'd ever had from people I loved. It was strange. It reminded me of the wind at the train station when I arrived for my second stay with them. Another sign which pushed me to trust more in my feelings.

I had to take the train to Paris and then another straight to Yvetot. Raphael's village was just a few kilometres away. But it wasn't so easy to reach my destination. After arriving in Bercy Station, in Paris, I had to take the metro to Paris St-Lazare. I was late, and the last train was already gone, so I had to wait till the next morning. I bought the ticket and waited on the bench, thinking about where I could spend the night. I didn't have too much money left, so I decided to spend the night in the train station. It was seven o'clock, and I saw hundreds of people passing through the station. After ten o'clock, fewer people moved through. I was tired, and I tried to sleep.

After a while, some officers arrived.

'Good evening, mister,' one of them said.

'Good evening,' I answered.

I was a bit afraid they would ask to see my ID, but the only thing they said was a warning: 'If you plan to spend the night here, we suggest you do not! First, because it's prohibited, but, even if we let you stay here, your safety will be at risk. There are some cheap hostels around here where you can spend the night.'

'I don't have too much money left. Is it possible to spend the night here? I'm not worried about risks; I never think about that. It's just for one night. Can I stay, please?'

'OK, we can make an exception for tonight, but you have to know that we are not responsible if someone steals your stuff—or maybe even worse. Is that clear? Enjoy your evening.'

I sat on the bench and I fell asleep, without caring about any problems. I was so tired.'

'Just look at him! Poor guy, he's still sleeping like a bear. We should pee on him; maybe he'll wake up then. Ha ha ha ha!'

After hearing these words, I woke up to see five black people around me. Worst of all, my suitcase was gone, and a big fat guy with shaved head was holding my backpack.

'Where is my suitcase?! Give my backpack, you shit, you f—!'

I didn't finish the word because I felt a punch in the back of my head. Maybe I shouldn't say that, but all I could think about was that my passport and all my stuff were gone with my suitcase. The punch was just the beginning, and then some kicks followed. I fell down and could only protect my face. I didn't want to go to Raphael's house with an ugly face. The attack didn't even last a minute, and then they ran away. It was over, but thinking that all my stuff was gone felt like the nightmare had just started.

I checked my pocket, and my wallet was gone. Hopefully, I would find my ticket on the bench. The ticket was there. After all they'd done to me, at least I could still get to my next destination. I felt pain throughout my entire body.

I arrived at the station at nine o'clock, and I started asking people about Chateau de Lumière. It was not more than seven kilometres away. I could walk twenty kilometres before my present condition, but after all those kicks, seven kilometres felt like a hundred. After walking for four hours, I arrived at the village church, and asked for directions again. Three kilometres more, and I finally saw a sign that read, 'Chemin de Lumière'.

I saw a big gate, high trees along the path, and the castle at the end of the path. I went inside and saw a big garden on the right side, full of apples. It was a bit difficult to believe that I was going to stay in such a beautiful house; even in my dreams I hadn't seen such a house.

I was looking around the castle, and I went to the right side because the front door was closed. I heard a voice talking on the phone.

Assuming it was my host, I called out, 'Hello, Raphael! Happy to see you!'

'Ah! Hello, Martin. Come in, please. Good to see you! I was waiting for you. Grab your stuff. I'm gonna show your room, but it's just for a few days. After that, you'll have to change; I'm waiting for many tourists who'll arrive soon.'

Two black Dobermans were sleeping near the chimney.

We went upstairs, and Raphael opened a door and said, 'Here it is. It's called the Pink Room; you can see for yourself why.'

I saw the colour pink everywhere, apart from the green view through the window.

'Martin, where did you leave your suitcase?'

'Mm … I have an interesting story to tell about this, Raphael.'

'I can't imagine what happened. First, we will drink something downstairs while I prepare lunch.'

I told Raphael the truth, and I could see in his face that he felt sorry for me.

'These days, you shouldn't take the risk of sleeping in a train station or a public place, Martin. The police were right. But don't worry. You are from another country, and you don't know the situation here in France, especially in Paris. Now, in France, something is stolen every ninety seconds; this is the highest rate of theft in French history. It's horrible! France is not France any more. The face of Paris has changed because of the refugees—I mean, the bad ones. No worries for you, though. You help me around the house, and I'm gonna help you to get some new stuff that you need.'

I entered the kitchen and saw a lot of things on the table. I could smell the aroma of beef cooking.

Raphael asked me to get the butter out of the fridge.

When I opened the fridge, I saw it was full.

'Difficult to find the butter in here, Raphael.'

'Ha ha. Don't worry, Martin; I'll get it myself,' Raphael said. 'You will get used to seeing a lot of stuff around, as I this is a B & B. I need to have what clients ask me for. Sometimes I even offer them dinner, but only in special cases.'

It is normal in France to eat healthy food. I could see four different kinds of cheese on the table. I knew that there were more than three hundred varieties of cheese available in France.

Raphael was a great cook, and I had no complaints.

After lunch, we went outside, and the dogs followed us.

'The bigger one is called Soia, and she's blind. Be careful to never leave her alone outside; she could easily get lost,' Raphael said. 'The other one is called Fils. Let me show you what you have to do next week. The apples in front need to be harvested soon, but before that, I want you to start to paint the windows of the castle—if you are not afraid of heights, of course.'

'No problem, Raphael. I'll make your windows look brand new. Painting is my specialty,' I said.

'Happy to hear that, young man! One of the most important things to do in this house is to take care of the guests. Help me serve breakfast, and have nice conversations with them. I hope you know basic English. Do you?'

'I have a degree in French language, and I can speak, English, Italian and a bit of Spanish.'

'Good to have you here, Martin. Another thing! Today is your first day, and seeing your condition, I suggest you rest now. Later, you can take Soia for a walk, to let you discover more about this place.'

I fell down on the bed like a dead man. I slept for four hours and, when I woke up, I opened the window and felt the fresh air. I felt no more pain for the moment. It was like waking up from a nightmare and then living in a beautiful dream surrounded by the colour pink—the colour of love.

I started to have a look inside the castle. Each room was a different colour: the Blue Room, the Green Room, the Gold Room (which was for the first-class guests).

I took Soia, as Raphael had suggested. After one hour of walking, I came back to the castle. Raphael was outside talking to some tourists who had just arrived.

'Martin, can you help them to take their luggage upstairs, please?'

'OK, no problem.'

After I brought their suitcases upstairs, they gave me ten euros. As I was working as a volunteer, I wanted to give the money to Raphael, but he said that I could keep any tips I received.

'Keep it, Martin; it's yours. I'm gonna ask you to do more than just serve the tourists. Of course, you will have your reward. Tomorrow, after serving, you can start the painting.'

During dinner, I saw an interesting documentary about the most-visited monuments in France by French people. On top of the list was Mont St-Michel. After studying this country for three years, I had never heard about this amazing masterpiece. I became directly curious.

'It was more than a three-hour drive from here!' Raphael said. 'It will be difficult to find enough free time to drive all the way there, but I promise I'll drive you to some nice places around here over the next few days. They're not as grand as Mont St-Michel, but I'm sure you'll not be disappointed.'

Because I was so attracted to Mont St-Michel, I decided to find some hosts nearby. I started to write to someone just thirty kilometres from it. She was called Ruby. Originally from Australia, she was asking for help in building works. I sent her an email, and I got the answer I wanted the very next day.

I woke up at seven o'clock the next morning. Raphael had already gone to get the fresh baguettes for breakfast. When he returned, we set the table. It was the best breakfast I ever had.

It was interesting to hear the stories of people coming from different countries, and my ability to speak several languages allowed me to tell them mine.

Raphael was happy with my presence there; I could easily see it in his eyes.

After breakfast, I started to paint the windows.

'Martin! Do you see the window that is closed?'

'Yes.'

'It's broken; that's why it's closed. I want you to make a fake one,' Raphael explained. 'We'll take the measurements, and then you're gonna paint it on a metal piece.'

After three hours of painting, it was time for lunch.'

'Do not continue with any more painting today. We'll visit Rouen, where I'm gonna buy some furniture as well,' said Raphael as he opened a bottle of aged wine.

Rouen—where Jeanne d'Arc spent her lasts days before being burned at the stake. In my last exam, there was a question about her, and now I was just a few metres away from the place where she died. Further on was the oldest hostel in France, built in the fourteenth century. After visiting the cathedral, Raphael suggested that we also visit the Aître St-Maclou, an old cemetery with the remains of thousands of people killed by the phenomenon of La Peste, in 1348. Rouen became one of my favourite towns in France, with its traditional old-style houses and tight paths.

'You see these old houses, Martin?' Raphael said. 'Look at their foundations. See how tight they are? Look at how the houses go up and become larger and larger. People in that time were smart to pay less money for the space, building big houses with smaller bases.'

We bought the furniture and then went back to the castle. Outside were a British couple who had just arrived by bike. When we started to get the furniture out of the car, they asked Raphael about the price.

'This chair cost forty euros, and it looks brand new!' said Raphael as he put down the regal-looking chair.

'Really? Are you serious? You could sell that chair for ten times that amount in London!'

Even to me the prices Raphael had paid were too low for the quality of the furniture. I was thinking about a future business: buying furniture here and selling it in richer countries and cities like Amsterdam, London, or even Switzerland.

During the days that followed, Raphael showed me some interesting places like Étretat. The view of the cliff from the top of the church became my favourite. Fécamp was interesting as well, but I was a bit disappointed with Le Havre, an industrial town that was less attractive.

'You don't see traditional houses here because this town was totally bombarded by the British Army during the Second World War, as it was occupied by German troops,' explained Raphael.

'Ah, another thing. Remind me that in two days it will be Shrimp Feast; there's no better place than Honfleur to celebrate it.'

I was having so much fun with Raphael. An old man living alone with all that wealth, he didn't care about spending money, showing me around and taking me to eat in expensive restaurants.

I was working more than five hours a day to prove my worth, and I didn't feel tired at all.

One afternoon, I was just going outside for a walk.

Raphael called out to me, saying, 'Martin, wait. I suggest you not forget to see the oldest oak tree in Europe. If you are curious, it's just a few kilometres from here. I'll give you a map, and you can take the bike.'

Every day, there was a new thing to see, and the time was passing so fast. In the last days, I bought clothes and shoes, and Raphael paid for everything. I almost finished the windows, and the last one I did was the fake window painted on a metal piece. After putting it in place, the result was magnificent.

Raphael was very happy. We drove around, and Raphael kept stopping, just to see if there was any difference when comparing the fake one with other windows. Difficult to find it.

He paid me five hundred euros, in cash, for my work. I hadn't expected this. It was bit too much for me, but Raphael insisted, so I put the envelope with the money in my pocket.

'Remember, you are always welcome, Martin!' Raphael told me when I left. 'I wish you could stay longer, but I know you have other plans for your future. If you ever need anything, do not hesitate to call me or to come straight here. Good luck!'

It was easy to find someone to carpool with till Rennes. I took the bus till the outskirts of the city, hoping someone would pick me up hitch-hiking after that. The place I was going to was called Les Maisons du Bois, in the village of Taden. It was getting dark, and I waited more than forty minutes on side of the road. A hunter stopped his car and drove me just a few kilometres. I started hitch-hiking again, but it was even more difficult this time. I not on the main road. The cars were few and far between, and the drivers seemed a bit more suspicious of picking up a stranger. Just as I was about to lose hope, someone driving a VW Golf stopped. He used GPS to check the address I gave him, and I saw that my destination was still half an hour away, in another direction.

But, after I explained my situation, he said, 'OK, I'm gonna drive you to the village, and then you'll be on your own to find the place where you're headed. It's not a good idea to leave someone outside these days with a big suitcase like yours. I'm a poker player, and I'm on my way to the casino. Poker is my second job, and I earn much more from it than my real job. I hope you are not afraid of high speed; I have to drive faster because I don't want to be late.'

He was driving two hundred kilometres per hour, and we arrived in the village in fifteen minutes.

'Now I have to leave you here. Good luck, mate!' he said as he dropped me off.

'May the cards go your way! Thanks a lot!' I said

It was almost midnight as I started walking across the village. Everything was quiet. I had the address, but I couldn't find anyone to ask for directions. I just walked and walked, in the dark, pulling my suitcase. I saw a house with lights on, and someone came out.

I didn't know what to say, so I just screamed, 'Hey!'

He didn't hear and just went back inside. I approached the gate and rang the bell. The same person came out again.

'Good evening, mister!' I said. 'Sorry for disturbing you so late, but I'm really lost. I can't find this address, and there's no one else to ask.'

'No worries,' he said. 'I don't call this a disturbance, as I wasn't sleeping. Let me have a look. Les Maisons du Bois. After another 50 metres, you have to take a right and then just go straight. It's not far from here.'

'Thanks a lot,' I said. 'That's very helpful; I was totally lost.'

I walked on. Five minutes later, a car approached. The driver was the person I had just spoken to.

He got out of the car and said, 'Sorry, mate! I gave you the wrong directions. I just checked on Google maps, and I saw that where you want to go is in another direction. Get in; I'll take you there.'

After three minutes of driving, we saw the sing indicating, 'Les Maisons du Bois.'

'Here we are!' he said. 'I have to leave you now. If you want to have a drink in the next few days, come to my house. You can tell me more about your traveling. It sounds really interesting.'

'Sure! Thanks for your help. Have a nice night!'

I went inside and saw a lot of stuff in the garden, including a concrete mixer and a lot of construction material. I could see that I was in the right place.

I rang the bell just one time, so as to not disturb anyone. Maybe people were asleep even though the lights were on.

After a minute, a girl came out. 'Hi! You are Martin, right?'

'Yes,' I answered.

I said this much joy, having finally arrived.

'Come in,' she said. 'My name's Katherine. We were waiting for you, but I think the others are sleeping now. There are some desserts on the table if you are hungry.'

Katherine was a blonde from US. Another helper, and she said were two others in the house. She showed me my room in another building next to the main building.

'This is your room, Martin,' Katherine said. 'The bathroom is over there, on the left. We usually wake up at nine o'clock to have breakfast, but since it is your first day here, Ruby said you can sleep in and wake up a bit later. She will explain your duties tomorrow. Goodnight!'

'Goodnight, Katherine! Thanks,' I said.

I woke up before nine o'clock, and I didn't want to sleep any longer. After brushing my teeth, I walked out of the bathroom. Someone was waiting right in front of the door.

'Good morning!' he said. 'So, you are the new one, eh? My name's Samuel, and I come from Spain.'

'Hi! My name's Martin; I'm from Albania.'

When I went to the kitchen, I met Ana, another helper, from Germany.

Ruby arrived two minutes later. 'Hi, and welcome to the family, Martin! Good to see you!'

'Hi, Ruby. Happy to be here, and thank you for accepting my request.'

Breakfast lasted a bit longer than I expected. I told Ruby about my way of travelling and the circumstances surrounding the loss of my passport.

'I'm really sorry to hear about your troubles, Martin, but it's good that you met Raphael. He gave you such nice help afterwards,' Ruby said. 'Tell me more about your plans. How long do you want to stay here?'

'I was having an adventure, and I didn't have a concrete idea about my travels. After losing all my papers, I felt totally lost. I don't yet know how long I want to stay here, Ruby. The reason I came here was to see Mont St-Michel,' I replied.

'Of course,' Ruby said. 'I'm gonna drive you over there one day, but I need to know the amount of time you plan to spend in our house. As you see, there's a lot of work to do, and I would like to accept someone else once you leave.'

'Give me a bit of time, please, to write to some hosts. In another three days, I'll be able to decide how long I want to stay. I already saw everything I wanted to see in France—once I get to Mont St-Michel—but my situation will make it difficult for me to travel to another country in Europe.'

'I'm not making any suggestions, but to move within the Schengen area you don't need a passport unless you go by plane or boat—at least that's my understanding.'

'Really?! I didn't know. Can I get caught by police?' I asked, really astonished.

'Well, if you think about getting caught, it can happen even inside the country,' Ruby said. 'But it's been a long time now that borders no longer exist.'

This was big news to me. I was instantly inspired to travel to all the countries I wanted to visit.

Ruby then explained the work I had to do in the attic: isolating the roof, gluing the paper, and so on. Easy work even though I was doing it for the first time—and especially because I was now so excited by Ruby's explanation of the Schengen area.

Samuel was working nearby, doing something else. I could practice my poor Spanish with him.

'Do you have any plan for your future, Martin, or are you travelling just for fun?' he asked.

'I think I'm gonna change plans about my travels. I'm gonna go to a different country after leaving Ruby's house. Why not Belgium? Maybe I can find some work there. I travel doing work exchange because it's a way for me to survive, but it would be easier if I had permission to work. I mean, you automatically have permission because Spain is part of EU, but Albania is not.'

'Belgium might be better than France,' Samuel said. 'But if you want to earn money, why not pick one of the richer countries like Luxembourg, Switzerland or Norway?'

'I have thought about that, Samuel; thanks for the suggestion. If I had to choose between these countries, I would choose Norway. I like the wild nature there, but I will stop wherever I find a real job—it doesn't matter which country.'

'Finding a job can be a bit difficult in your situation, Martin. Wishing you luck is the only help I can give you. I can work almost anywhere in Europe, and I think it's still hard. That's why I prefer work exchange for the moment; after leaving Spain, I don't have the energy to search for something else.'

At one o'clock lunch was already waiting outside in the garden. I met another guy living in the house. He was called Basil, and he came from Greece. Albanians do not have a good reputation in that country, nor do they with us, but Basil became my best friend immediately, and I was for him as well. He wasn't a helper but an employee working for Ruby's husband. After lunch, we went back to work for another two hours.

That afternoon, we drove to a small harbour, where I met Josephine, a seal one metre long, very quiet and soft.

'Do not be curious to touch her skin, Martin. She's very sensitive and might bite you,' said Basil.

Ten years ago, Josephine was rescued by people who found her on the coast, abandoned and hurt. After her rescue, she never left this place and became a very friendly animal for both residents and tourists.

After sunset and some selfies, we went back to the house. I could already smell the aroma of the excellent meal that Katherine had prepared. The helpers' duties were split, and cooking was her speciality.

The next days were very enjoyable, with good company and easy work most of the time. Whenever things got more complicated, I could ask for Samuel's help. He was also generous about teaching me some Spanish.

When the weekend came, we decided to visit Mont St-Michel, the reason I had come to that area. Basil drove, and we reached our destination in forty minutes. We parked the car, but the island was still a distance away. The two-kilometre walk was nothing with that amazing view in front of us.

I can describe Mont St-Michel in just one word: *masterpiece.* This is why it is protected by UNESCO and part of the World Heritage Sites. At the base of the monastery and just outside its walls were houses for farmers and fishermen. A lot of tourists filling all the nearby stores and restaurants. I went with Basil and introduced myself as a Greek without ID, so I didn't have to pay the admission fee. Tourists from non-EU countries had to pay fifteen euros to enter. After two hours of visiting the large interior halls, we made our way to the long exterior balcony. I couldn't call it an island at that moment; it was just sand all around, with some people walking on it. The shifting sand could be dangerous, swallowing people, but not when you had an experienced guide. We saw what we wanted and then went back to the base of the building, where we'd started. To end this exciting day, we went to a restaurant in Dinan, a small old town not far from where we were staying. I didn't care too much about spending some money; thanks to Raphael, I still had enough to continue travelling.

I started to write emails to some hosts in southern Belgium and in Luxembourg. The next day, I got an answer from someone in Belgium. She was called Marianne; she lived alone in a village and wanted help in the garden. I told Ruby when I planned to leave, and she suggested that I carpool till Rance.

'So, you're gonna stay here just three more days, Martin. I wish you could stay longer with us, and I want to remind you that you are welcome to come back. It's been such a big pleasure to have you here,' said Ruby.

'Thanks a lot, Ruby,' I said. 'It gives me hope and joy to hear that before leaving.'

'One last thing, Martin. I'll give you a day off tomorrow. Basil will drive you in my car to St-Malo. It's a beautiful town you should not miss before leaving.'

'Having such a good company and seeing all those nice places around, my three days there passed like three hours. I was sorry that I was leaving, but I had to follow my plan. My final destination was now Norway. If I wanted to earn money, why not go to the richest country?

'You are the first Albanian I ever loved,' said Basil, after giving me a hug.

Of course, he met a lot of Albanians in his country. Maybe some of them could call him gay for what he said, but no one had ever said those words to me before, and I really appreciated hearing them.

Ruby had already found someone for me to carpool with till Rance. The driver came half an hour late, but at least I didn't miss it.

After arriving in Rance, I took the train to my destination. Some officers entered the train car, looking for someone who didn't have a ticket. I was a bit afraid of being checked, since I didn't have a passport, but all they asked was to see my ticket. I got out at the station, where Marianne was waiting. I didn't see any picture of her prior, so I hoped she could recognize me first. A black lady around fifty years old stood a few metres away, smiling. I didn't know she was black. I was a bit surprised, just because she was my first black host, but it turned out I was her first volunteer.

'Good to see you, Martin!' Marianne said as I approached.

'Happy to see you, Marianne. I hope you didn't have to wait for too long.'

'No, I just arrived. You can bring your suitcase along. I hope you don't mind some shopping before going home, and then we'll make dinner.'

'Cooking is not my specialty, Marianne, but I can help.'

'No worries, Martin; you can just sit and relax. I'm sure you are tired after the long trip from Bretagne.'

Breuillet looked like a lost village. It was in Ardennes, in southern Belgium, with a lot of history of the Second World War. Marianne said hundreds of thousands of Germans were killed and buried in this area.

Her house was small and old, with a tiny kitchen and some renovation work half complete.

'Sorry for the mess, Martin. As I plan to sell the house, I want to do some renovations first. It's difficult to sell an old house around here. The young are the only ones left here,' Marianne said, adding, 'So, tell me more about yourself.'

I told her my story while she cooked dinner.

'Well, son, first, I have to congratulate you for your courage. I hope you will find your destiny. I see you are on the right path. I'm a traveller as well. I often go to Asia, mostly in India, where my master is. I have learned a lot from my master, and he has a master himself. Are you curious to know how he became his master?'

'Tell me,' I answered, since I was curious.

'When he first met his master, he vomited just beside his legs, and my master felt very disgusted. But then, in the same place, a beautiful rose mallow grew—you know, those flowers you find often in the swamps.'

'I understand how beautiful things can be born from dirty places or circumstances,' I said, thinking about my own story and being optimistic at the same time.

'If you plan to travel Asia, I suggest Tibet, the highest region on earth. I have been there twice, and I found it very special. The inhabitants stay very close to each other and share everything. It's not easy to survive in an elevation of five thousand metres, where even breathing is difficult, but it is a special sensation—even more so after leaving that place,' Marianne said and then added, 'And if you plan to visit India, you have to get used to the monkey thieves. This is another interesting thing about my second life there. Apart from stealing, they can be even dangerous, challenging you.'

'Really? How?' I asked.

'Sometimes, the moment you go out from your door, they make a circle, and the biggest of them come to challenge you. It is smart to make noise, banging things, to show them you are tough and not afraid, and then they leave.'

It was eleven o'clock at night when Marianne showed me my bedroom.

'Usually I wake up at eight o'clock, and I start with meditation. I'm not suggesting that you join me tomorrow, Martin. As you are tired, you can sleep until later. After breakfast, I'm gonna show you the work in the garden. Goodnight, son. Sleep well!'

'Goodnight, Marianne, and thank you.'

The only work Marianne needed in the garden was just to harvest a big apple tree, cut the grass, and do some planting.

'This is all work you need, Marianne?'

'After collecting all the apples, we're gonna make juice,' Marianne explained.

I got an answer from hosts in Luxembourg, but they needed me in three weeks. Marianne's work wouldn't last more than a week. I had to be fast and write to someone else nearby. Just a few hours later, I received the answer I wanted from a mother and son, Christine and Damian, living in a village close to Brussels.

The next day, Marianne proposed a visit to her friend who lived nearby.

'She's called Bernadette,' Marianne said. 'She drinks a lot, but she's a lovely person. She's a sculptor and has three kids. Her husband travels a lot in his camping car during her crisis time.'

We walked for fifteen minutes and arrived at an old house. Bernadette was outside, working.

'Hello, Marianne,' she said. 'Glad to see you! Where have you been all this time? I missed you!'

Bernadette looked more like a witch than a drunk person, but I smelled alcohol as she approached me. While she kissed my face, I had to hold my breath for a few seconds.

'And who's this handsome boy? Where do you come from, sweetheart?' asked Bernadette, looking into my eyes.

'Hi! My name's Martin.'

'Martin is my guest and helping me in the garden. He's doing such nice work, and it's sad that he's gonna leave soon,' said Marianne.

'If he wants to stay longer, he doesn't have to leave, Marianne. I have a lot of work to do in my house. But first, we go inside and talk. I have brought some good wine from France,' said Bernadette, touching my shoulder.

'What kind of help do you need, Bernadette?' asked Marianne, being curious.

'Well, he can transport my statues from one place to another,' answered Bernadette, smiling.

It was evident she wanted sex, but I didn't want to give my dick to an old drunk lady who smelled of alcohol.

I didn't enjoy that visit very much, and I was happy to leave after an hour. Maybe Marianne wanted to stay longer, but she understood that I was getting really bored.

'Sorry, Martin,' Marianne said. 'We went at the wrong time. She's nicer when she's not drinking.'

The week passed too fast at Marianne's house. After making the juice, she gave me fifty euros for the nice job I did. In truth, I worked a bit harder than she'd expected, and she was very satisfied with her first volunteer.

I said goodbye to Marianne and went on to my next destination.

Christine was waiting at the train station when I arrived. She seemed a bit old, but when she told me she was 70 I couldn't believe it—I had thought she was about 50.

'I need some help in the garden, Martin,' Christine explained. 'As I'm old, I can't do it all myself, and Damian is busy travelling. I have some other projects too. We'll talk during dinner time and then decide how long you want to stay.'

The house was modern, mixed with wood and stones. I could see candles everywhere inside the house.

'As you see, Martin, we prefer candles to lamps. I present to you Tito, our dog.'

Tito was a dachshund, and he couldn't stop trying to lick my face from our first meeting.

'Do you like dogs, Martin? I hope you aren't allergic.'

'I love dogs, Christine,' I answered, petting the dog.

'I'm asking because I had a Chinese girl as a helper last year, and she was really afraid. I list the dog in my profile description, so people should know with whom and what they're gonna live, even for a short time, in order to adapt easily. Some of them, I think, just see some nice pictures and then directly send an email.'

There was a knock at the door.

'This must be Damian. Please open the door, Martin.'

I opened the door and saw a guy wearing a sportive jacket. He had black hair and was a bit taller than me.

'You must be Martin. My name's Damian; I think you know that already.'

'Nice to meet you, Damian. Yes, of course, I know your name.'

'Sit at the table, guys. Dinner is almost ready,' said Christine.

Christine explained to me the work she wanted in the garden: easy things like cutting branches and digging a trench around the garden and then filling the trench with stones.

'I don't expect too much from this work exchange, Martin, not more than four hours per day, but I want you to do the work well,' Christine said. 'The Chinese girl was very sweet, but I was a bit disappointed with her work, as she didn't have even the slightest experience doing garden work.'

'During my travels, I have done a lot of gardening. I enjoy it a lot; it's more like therapy than work. You give me a task, and I'll try to do better than you expect,' I assured Christine, secure in my experience with gardening.

Christine told me about her prior life. She had three different husbands. Damian later explained to me that her third husband had died peacefully some years before, so Damian had been taking care of his mother for a long time.

'We don't work, Martin. I get a pension from Switzerland, and Damian just takes care of small business,' continued Christine.

'I have some good connections with big brands. I know people with a lot of money who want to launder it by opening a business. That's when I intervene, making the necessary arrangements. I don't earn too much, but I have some plans to create my own business, a small one of course. I plan to build a storehouse in the garden. I have a friend in Italy, a kind of collector. It's a crisis there, and the value of artwork is going down. The next step is to sell all this art in richer countries, but first I have to bring the collection here. After that, I can go step by step,' said Damian.

I was glad to meet someone talking about real business. I told Damian about my future business with furniture in Normandy.

'Try to get your papers sorted first, and then maybe I can help you!' he said.

'It's just a vision,' I said. 'For now, I'm planning to go to Norway, the richest country in Europe.'

'Yes, I have heard about Norway,' Damian said. 'Go there! I know someone who wants to go to northern Norway, to an island called Svalbard. It's very wild and freakin' cold, but you can find work there even without papers.'

'Really?!'

'Do not be so excited, Martin. Given your situation, it cannot be easy to get there.'

'I'll not stop trying,' said.

The dinner was really enjoyable. Afterwards, Christine showed me the room where I would stay.

The next morning, I woke up at nine and started working in the garden. I did a bit more than four hours, as was my habit. Christine was happy to get more than she'd expected.

'Martin, I'm really surprised how fast you made that. I think I have been lucky this time, getting someone like you,' she said.

I always worked hard, and I didn't care that I gave more than expected; I did it just to hear some kind words. Of course, I wasn't disappointed with all the delicious food.

My stay with Christine and Damian didn't last as long as expected. After a week, I had finished what they asked me to do, and they were very satisfied.

'We are very happy with you here, Martin. I wish you could stay longer. I was expecting you to finish all this in two weeks, and you did it just in one. That's incredible!' said Christine.

'We're gonna propose something more,' Damian said. 'Look, I want to help you, Martin. If you agree to paint two rooms upstairs, we will pay you for your work. I know you are good at painting, but you have to remove all the wallpaper first, repair the walls with plaster and cement, clean them with sandpaper, and then paint them. If you can do all that, just tell me how much you would want per hour.'

'I'm here as a volunteer,' I said. 'Thank you for your offer; it is very generous, but I would like you to decide how much to pay me; you can give me as much as you want. You know that I'm not searching to make money but opportunities.'

I thought that I was doing him a favour; maybe he would offer me something more than pocket money. There's no big difference between getting paid three hundred euros or twice that. For me, it is the same, as these small amounts can't make any real difference. If I wanted to earn money, I would like to talk about some real cash.

Taking off the paper was an embarrassing job, and it was the first time I had repaired walls with plaster or cement. But I did it all professionally after watching some videos on YouTube.

'I really like your way of doing things, Martin. I would like to talk with you about something serious, but let's keep it a secret,' said Damian as he served me a glass of whisky.

'Just trust me, Damian; I'm ready for anything.'

'I have a friend living in Marseilles, France. He used to work for a company in Algeria, digging an underground tunnel. While working, they found an ancient village, and the most important thing discovered was the head of a god from a statue, valued at not less than two million euros. We are searching for a collector, but it's really difficult to find it for something illegal. During your trip, maybe you can find someone to make the deal, and then, of course, you will have a share in the sale.'

At the beginning, I remained surprised, but as I thought about it, it became more difficult to believe it. I worked ten hours per day; I didn't have the time to even go for a walk outside, apart from the weekend.

It started to get colder at the end of October. I had to borrow Damian's jacket when I wanted to go outside. After a few times, he came home with a new jacket as a gift for me. The next day, he gave me a pair of Adidas shoes—my favourite brand—and some clothes as well.

After two weeks of hard work, I finished both of rooms. The result was perfect.

'Martin, I have another gift for you, but first, you have to wash your hands,' said Damian.

We went upstairs, and he showed me a Dolce and Gabbana summer suit. Giving me all those extravagant gifts was his way of letting me know that I would not be paid too much in cash.

I already had an appointment with the next host, at Arlon, not far from their village.

We ate our last lunch together in a restaurant. During our conversation, Christine put an envelope on the table.

'This is for you, Martin, for all the hard work you did. We are very satisfied,' said Christine, encouraging me to open the envelope.

'Thanks a lot for everything,' I said.

'It's not too much, Martin,' said Damian.

I knew that already after receiving all those gifts. That's why I just said, 'This is an exchange of volunteer work, so it doesn't matter to me how much is inside the envelope; I'm happy with whatever it is.'

I opened the envelope on the way to Arlon: just two hundred euros. I was disappointed after all those nice moments I passed with them. It could have been just a bit more, and that would have made a difference. True, Damian had asked me what hourly wage I wanted, but I wanted to see what they would pay me on their own. They had seemed the best for me, but were they really? No, because the best people in the world do not exist. I was travelling to understand more about people, not to earn money—at least not for the moment. For me, it was enough just to arrive at the next destination.

At the Arlon station, I had to wait not less than forty-five minutes.

'Hello! My name's Manfred. Sorry for being late,' my new host said. 'You must be Martin, right? I saw your profile picture before going out, and I turned my car around twice because I didn't notice you in the middle of that crowd.'

'Ah! Sorry, Manfred. I didn't notice you either!'

Manfred wanted to go shopping before returning to the house and suggested that I accompany him. What impressed me most were his bags filled with spaghetti and macaroni.

'I love spaghetti, Martin, and I don't eat more than once a day!' he explained.

For the moment, I thought I was going to have to eat the same way he did.

Maybe he read my mind because he then said, 'Not you, Martin; you're gonna eat three meals every day. I'm just talking about myself. I have to diet because I'm very fat.'

He wasn't really fat, maybe a bit heavier than average, but his kind of diet seemed unusual.

Manfred spoke to me in French, having read my profile, and we decided to continue speaking in this language.

'It will be better for my kids if we speak French, Martin. They learn German in school first, and then, at 9 years old, they start with French, which is the official language, so it's used in government—if you want to get working papers, for example.'

'Do you have your own language?' I asked.

'Yes, of course! We call it Luxembourgeois.'

We arrived at the house, and Manfred showed me a caravan in the garden, which was where I would sleep.

'You'll just use the caravan for sleeping,' Manfred explained. 'All the meals will be served inside the house. Of course, you can use the TV and whatever else you need. I suggest you to turn on the heat in the caravan, as it's getting colder now.'

I didn't see any difference between the rooms I'd stayed in with other hosts and that caravan where I stayed for three weeks. I had plenty of space, two beds, one small kitchen, and a tiny bathroom that I never used. The only problem was the heating system, which wasn't powerful enough to properly heat the caravan. Covering myself with enough blankets while sleeping at night was the solution. The rest of time I spent inside their house, which was nice and warm.

First, I met nine-year-old Ben, Manfred's youngest, and then his twelve-year-old daughter, Hanna. I met his wife, Julia, when she came home later on.

Julia immediately explained to me everything that I would use inside the house. In work exchange it was normal for the family to introduce themselves and then go over the house rules.

'Here's my room. You can use it while I'm not here if you want a bit more privacy,' suggested Manfred, showing me his personal computer as well.

Manfred and Julia didn't sleep together even when they were young, a second strange fact to learn about him after already knowing about his abnormal diet.

The next morning, I woke up at half past seven and ate breakfast.

Afterwards, Julia took a semitruck full of empty crates.

'The fields where we're gonna work are just a kilometre away, but I always use the truck to get the vegetables I need for the house and the clients,' Julia explained. 'We have a big fridge inside the barn, which we use like a moving store; I mean, my husband drives it around the village to sell vegetables. The clients are mostly old people—or rich ones who are too lazy to go to the supermarket, and then, of course, we sell them at a higher price. The work will consist mostly of harvesting vegetables and then washing and cutting them.'

The barn was huge and modern. Inside were three tractors and a luxurious van with the fridge connected behind it.

'If you need to use the toilet, Martin, you can find it on the left of the entrance. Today, the work will consist of harvesting cauliflower, taking off the dead leaves, and washing the cauliflower. Afterwards, I'm gonna help you put them in the crates inside the fridge. If you have any question, please do not hesitate to ask me; I'll be in the fields harvesting something else,' said Julia, bringing me some work clothes and boots.

We returned home at around one o'clock in the afternoon, a time which became our routine. I was getting bored with this; I wanted something more than just work exchange. I asked Julia if I could help her in the afternoon as well, hoping they would offer me a small payment for some extra hours. I was in one of the richest countries in Europe, and I wanted to earn some money. Instead of offering me any payment, Manfred made me work on Saturdays as well. I was eating spaghetti every day, and I understood that they spared expenses as much as possible in order to expand their own business. My time there became the poorest experience in the richest country.

I didn't hesitate to write to a new host; I wanted to go back to Belgium. The situation became more enjoyable when two German girls arrived as volunteers in the house, but that didn't last even a week. Charlie and Mia, two pretty blondes 17 and 18 years old, who'd just finished high school and now planned to travel through Europe for a year. Luxembourg was their second destination. They'd first visited a monastery in Belgium, and they described it as a magical place with a lot of positive energy.

'If you need a very peaceful and warm place, Martin, I suggest you visit the Sint Lucas Monastery in Halem. We were so lucky to visit this place first, surrounded by beautiful and open-minded people. If you want, I can give you their contact information,' Mia said, giving me their email address.

'Thank you, Mia, I'll keep it in mind. Given my situation, I always need an address to go to before leaving the place where I am.'

Fortunately, I'd already received a positive answer from a religious community called Hare Krishna, in Durbuy. Their profile description looked quiet fascinating, especially the pictures of a big castle with 120 people from all over the world living in it.

Julia brought me to the Arlon station late in the afternoon. I didn't want to miss the opportunity to visit Ardennes during my last day in Luxembourg. By nightfall, I was off to my next adventure.

3

HARE KRISHNA

It was getting dark when the train to Durbuy arrived. When I noticed the separate cars, it reminded me of the *Harry Potter* train. As a youngster, I was a big fan of those movies, always dreaming of being part of that imaginary life. I arrived at my stop at ten o'clock, and I didn't see anyone waiting for me in the train station. I didn't have the address because Work Exchange never included addresses in their profiles. I saw a pizzeria nearby, and I went in to ask how to get to Durbuy. They explained it was too far to walk there. I didn't leave the restaurant without getting a pizza with meat and mushrooms, as I would have to eat vegetarian while staying in the Hare Krishna castle—their first rule upon accepting any volunteers. I had never eaten vegetarian before; in fact, some Albanians wouldn't even know the word *vegetarian*.

I left the pizzeria just as a taxi van stopped nearby. A couple got out, and I saw the luxurious interior of the vehicle, complete with monitors.

'Good evening! How much does it cost to go to the Hare Krishna castle?' I said to the taxi driver. Of course, I expected a high price because of all that luxury inside.

'Twenty euros,' he said.

I gave him the money, even though I saw that my pockets were almost empty. I didn't want to stay outside on a cold night just to wait for a long walk the next day.

After a few minutes, the driver announced, 'We'll be there in about five minutes; it's only seven kilometres from here.'

Seven kilometres? I thought, surprised. I had imagined it was much further away. Twenty euros for a nine-minute drive was a lot of money, but I didn't say a word—I just enjoyed my short trip in that luxurious van.

He turned the car on the right side of the road, across from an old gate, and I could see the rear of the castle. He stopped near the guest house.

'OK, I'm gonna leave you here, son,' the taxi driver said. 'Enjoy your stay!'

Just as I put on my backpack, I saw someone exiting the castle.

'Hello!' I called. 'Sorry to bother you, but can I ask you something?'

'Yes, of course.'

'I came here via Work Exchange, and I don't know where I can leave my stuff. Maybe you could—'

'Ah, I'm a volunteer also,' he interjected. 'I can show you where to put your stuff. We all sleep up in the dormitory on the top floor of the guest house. My name's Kai. I'm from Boston.'

'My name's Martin. I'm from Albania.'

He looked to be about my age, though a bit shorter than me. He was kind enough to hold my backpack while I pulled my suitcase.

On the second floor, we passed someone with a shaved head, wearing some unusual clothes.

Maybe he's a monk, I thought.

'He's the boss here!' said Kai, laughing. 'I'm kidding. He's a devotee. His name's Mourad, and he's from Azerbaijan.

The dormitory was long, not less than fifteen metres, and full of people.

'As you see, Martin, apart from the noise and the bad smell, it's not bad. You can take a bed on the floor; there's one at the end of the room,' said Kai. 'The guy standing on your right is called Logan, and the other one is Simon—he came just two hours before you.'

'Hi, I come from New Zealand. And you are from?' asked Simon, being curious.

'Albania.'

Logan seemed a bit more serious. All he said was 'Hello.'

I took the bed near Mourad. At first, he seemed like a lunatic just out of prison, but I soon discovered his pure heart.

The next morning, I woke up at nine o'clock. I noticed that Kai was already gone. I brushed my teeth quickly and went to the castle. Fortunately, I met Mourad along the way, and he showed me the way: through the rear entrance, across the kitchen, down the long corridor, up a few steps, and into the big hall. There were a lot of people waiting in a long queue.

'Martin! Come here,' said Mourad. 'I'm gonna show you where the cupboard is. You can pick up a plate and the rest of what you need for breakfast.'

I waited in the queue with everyone else. Five devotees were serving breakfast. The first one was serving soup, but I declined, as it was too heavy for me first thing in the morning. The second was serving porridge, one of my favourites for breakfast, so I didn't hesitate to take two big spoons. The third one was serving the tea. The fourth gave out bread, jam, and butter. The last one was serving different fruits and some sweets.

After filling up my plate, I went to join Mourad and other devotees sitting inside the big room.

Before I entered, Mourad stopped me, saying, 'Please, Martin, take off your shoes before you step inside.'

In front of me was a blue statue of Krishna, lying on his side. He had four hands.

'Do you understand the meaning of the four hands, Martin?' asked Mourad.

I had no idea, so I shook my head.

'Because she's a hard-working girl! Ha ha!' Mourad laughed, and I noticed that half of his teeth were missing.

I had almost emptied my plate when an old lady appeared in front of me. She had white hair and blue eyes, and a blue cloak covered her. She leaned heavily on the stick she gripped with her right hand.

'Hare Krishna!' said the old lady, welcoming me.

'Hello!'

'My name's Baghavati, and I'm the director of this community. So, you must be the new volunteer, apart from the other new guy, from New Zealand, whom I just met outside.'

'Yes.'

'What's your name, and from where do you come from?'

'My name's Martin, and I come from Albania.'

'Well, I'm happy to have you here, Martin, and I hope you'll enjoy your stay with us. If you've finished breakfast, I suggest you join Josh. He's from Britain, and he's gonna explain the work to be done in the cowshed; we always start with that. First, milking the cows—'

'Metting?' I said, misunderstanding the word *milking.*

'Josh will explain everything. He is waiting for you at the rear of the castle, behind the kitchen where you came in,' continued Baghavati, this time in a more serious tone.

Josh was almost two metres tall, a real muscle guy around 30 years old. He spoke without a British accent, as he said he'd spent the last five years working in Australia.

When we arrived at the cowshed, Simon, Kai, and Logan were already there.

'Martin, grab a pitchfork and help Simon clean out the shit inside the fence,' said Josh. 'I hope you are not afraid of the cows. Just be careful: sometimes they can get angry and attack you, and watch your feet because they can step on you when they move.'

'It'll be better if you can bring some hay, Martin. I'm almost done in here,' called Simon.

'Come! I'm gonna show you where the hay is,' said Josh, pulling a towards the rear of the shed, where I saw some huge piles of hay.

The cowshed was divided into two parts: three bulls lay in one section, and two cows were in the other. I put the hay inside, while Simon and Kai milked the cows.

'You're gonna try it tomorrow, Martin; today, Simon the maniac is curious about touching cow tits for the first time,' said Kai.

After finishing in the cowshed, we went to the huge garden, which was filled with vegetables and flowers.

'OK, guys, now the plan is to take of everything rotten out of the ground and put it all in the compost pile over there,' said Logan, pointing to the pile. 'After cleaning the compost line, you have to collect some leaves at the other side, just in front of the castle where the big trees are. You're gonna use the wheelbarrow to bring the leaves here and put them on top of what you cleaned. One last piece of advice: If you see a spoilt, sick vegetable, throw it beside the compost, not inside, to reduce the risk of contaminating the entire compost.'

With that, Logan left.

'Hey, Kai, is Logan responsible for the volunteers?' I asked.

'Just for the moment. He's filling in for Harvey, who will be back in a few days, I heard,' answered Kai.

At half past one, Josh suggested we leave the tools inside the greenhouse because it was time for lunch.

We sat on the veranda at the rear of the castle. As always, they sang the song of Krishna before starting the meal.

Baghavati was at the head of the queue.

'Baghavati is a strange name. Maybe she has another one,' said Simon.

'Maybe she's really called Jessy or Linda,' said Kai, laughing.

'Keep your voice down, mate. This morning, she was angry, and I don't have even the slightest idea why,' whispered Logan. 'But if you want to know about names, all the directors of these communities are called Baghavati.'

Logan knew a lot about this environment and the people living here, for the simple reason that he'd already spent a year here, perhaps even longer.

'Hello! How are you guys doing?' said a tiny girl not more than a metre and a half tall. 'Sorry to interrupt. Ah, I see another volunteer here! My name's Niki.'

'Nice to meet you, Niki. My name's Martin.'

Niki told me she was from Taiwan.

'Are there any more volunteers here?' asked Simon.

'For the moment, just the six of us,' replied Logan. 'Tomorrow, another guy, from Spain, will arrive.'

The food was tasty and varied. I could accept being a vegetarian for a long time while living in the Krishna community. Indian food became one of my favourites.

'I love this food! I'll grab some more!' said Simon.

As he approached the baskets, Baghavati stopped him, saying, 'First, you have to wash your hands. It is a rule here: every time you put more food on your plate, you have to wash your hands again.'

We had a rest till four o'clock. Before that, I sat down in the reception to play with my smartphone.

Kai passed by and said, 'Hey, Martin, it is time for some cake! You can follow me if you like.'

We went inside a tiny kitchen filled with people. We each took a piece of cake and set off to a hidden place which Kai called the 'Chamber of Secrets'. There, I ate cake baked without eggs. It was the first time I'd ever tried such a cake—delicious!

We had just one hour to rest, from four o'clock till five. The sun was setting when Kai took Simon and me to the top of the tower. It was a beautiful view just before sunset. I could see the long flat fields of Ardennes. From up I noticed the shield shape of the yard just in front of the castle.

'OK, guys! I hope you enjoyed the view. I'll be waiting in the kitchen at seven o'clock for our last duty: preparing food for the cows and then milking them again,' said Kai.

At half past seven, we finished our last job. After that, it was time for dinner, which they called *pragmata*. As always, I heard the same words chanted through the corridors: 'Hare Krishna, Hare Rama.' People went back and forth, repeating these words for hours. As Logan had told us, most people came to the castle from a destructive past, and participating in this religion helped them to forget it. Becoming spiritual was always a big step towards positive self-improvement.

The next day, we followed the same routine. In the evening we met Manuel, a slender guy speaking with the lowest voice. Harvey came a day after, and he introduced us to a new work programme. His plan consisted of building *hugelkultur* beds in the garden.

'What are hugelkultur beds?' asked Simon.

'I'm gonna explain it to all of you. Hugelkultur is something we do often here in Belgium. First, you have to dig a trench twenty to thirty centimetres deep, in the same shape as other trenches are built. After that, you take some wood—make sure to take the biggest pieces first—and then you put some compost and leaves on it. Repeat the same thing several times till it reaches the same height as the other ones you see here. Put the earth you dug for the trench on top of the pile, and then cover it again with compost and leaves. Josh, Simon, and Logan will bring the compost from the cowshed, with some help from the oxen. Kai, Manuel, and Martin will dig the trench.'

Kai and I started digging, and Manuel cut the wood. It was hard work digging that trench—Harvey wanted it to be almost 12 metres long—and it took us a whole day to finish it.

That evening, we met Vade. He was from Holland, not a volunteer but someone with a big mouth, making a mess in the dormitory. Mourad explained the rules that everyone had to respect to keep it clean and tidy. Vade had arrived just one hour before, and he had already stolen someone else's towel, just because he didn't have one of his own.

I was lying down when Kai came to me and said, 'Hey, Martin, I'm going to have dinner. It's nine o'clock, and they put out some more food. I didn't find anything earlier. At half past seven, the kitchen was empty.'

'I'm hungry too!' screamed Simon. 'A bunch of black people were grabbing all that food before.'

Kai had it right. The baskets in the kitchen were full of food. In three minutes we almost emptied them, and then we went to sit in our secret room.

'You know what that crazy guy, Vade, told me?' said Kai.

'What?!' Simon and I asked at the same time.

'He said, "I'm going crazy because my wife just left me, but that savage bitch never understood that I was the best fucker in the village!" Ha ha!' said Kai.

'Ha ha ha!'

'Hello, ladies! Are you having some fun over here?' It was Josh, and Logan followed him.

'I'm lucky there's still something in the baskets!' screamed Logan.

We stayed there for almost two hours, just talking. When my turn came, I talked about the kind of sacrifices I was ready to ready to make while trying to become someone.

'You already are someone!' said Simon.

'We all are, Simon,' I said. 'But why not go back to my country in a Range Rover.'

'And how do you think you're gonna make all this money, Albanian?' asked Logan.

'I'm gonna rob a bank,' I said, not aware of his diabolical mind.

'Careful what you think, Albanian; it's not that easy to rob a bank these days! I come from a troubled past as well, but I never tried. I wouldn't take that kind of risk,' continued Logan.

'Come on, mate, don't be so serious. I was kidding!' I said.

The idea that I was among friends and speaking freely about things had raised my good sense of humour. I felt positive in such instances, even when confessing my unrealistic desires.

I came back to the guest house, and I saw Mourad in the corridor. I was curious to know more about the Hare Krishna religion, and I asked him if he could recommend a book about it.

'If you are a traveller, and you want to learn more about that spiritual life, I suggest the book *The Journey of Self-Discovery*, but I don't have for a copy of it at the moment. You have to go to the castle reception and ask for Dimitri, a Polish guy. Tell him that I sent you,' said Mourad in his typical good and kind way.

The next day, I went to see Dimitri. He gave me the book, which was small and thin.

Later, at half past three, I went to the kitchen for some cake, and I encountered Kai.

'Hey, Martin, a new volunteer just arrived,' Kai told me. 'She's from Brazil. Very hot! Too bad I have to leave in two days.'

'Cool! Can't wait to meet her,' I said. 'And good you are leaving, mate; one less rival makes it better and easier for me.'

'I hope you're gonna make it, but don't forget the other wolves around you,' said Kai. 'I don't feel sorry about leaving, since I'm going to Brussels. I have a friend studying there, and he knows a lot of girls to introduce me to.'

'Better for you!'

'Hey, where is my piece of cake?' screamed Simon.

'First, say hello, dude! There's no cake for a barker like you,' said Kai, laughing.

'Watch your mouth, Kai,' said Simon.

'I'm kidding! Don't be angry; there's a lot of cake on the table. Calm down,' said Kai in a low voice.

I took the biggest piece of cake, put it on a plate, and served it to Simon.

'Take it, Simon,' I said. 'It's all yours, but don't forget you owe me a big piece of cake like this one.'

'I didn't know Albanians were as smart and kind as you are, Martin,' said Simon.

'Thanks for the compliment!'

'Now you owe me a compliment!' answered Simon.

At five o'clock, after our rest, we began the work in the garden, filling the trench with wood, compost, and leaves.

Logan interrupted us, asking, 'Good job, guys; I see you're doing well. Did you see the Spanish guy, Manuel? He's been missing all day, and he didn't ask Harvey for a day off.'

'Yesterday as well,' offered Simon. 'He didn't join us in the cowshed.'

'OK! No worries; I'll discuss it with Harvey. Keep going. See you at dinner.'

With these words, Logan walked away.

That evening, I wasn't keen on seeing Logan any more, but I did want to say hello to the Brazilian girl. Kai was right: she was super hot—big breasts, brown eyes, long black hair, teeth white as snow. Her name was Milena. I couldn't believe that a girl like her would go and do volunteer work. I had the impression that she liked me just because she asked how long I would be there. I was interested in finding a way to become her boyfriend for the short period of time that I would be at the castle. Firstly, I added her on Facebook. I had to be fast about expressing something romantic to her, and sending her a message was simpler than saying it in front of her, as I wasn't used to doing that often. Besides, I didn't want to wait any more. Kai reminded me about the other wolves. Logan was attracted to Milena, so was Josh in his funny way, and Vade from Holland too. It became a band of wolves and dogs, but I wasn't worried, as Milena wanted to stay mostly with me.

The next morning, I was eating breakfast with Simon.

Baghavati came by and greeted us with 'Hare Krishna.'

Simon answered directly, 'Good morning!'

'Hare Krishna!' I answered, with my mouth full.

Baghavati didn't say anything else. She just threw a sideways glance at Simon and left.

I had to reproach him, as I was older (Simon was only 18 years old).

'I'm a Christian, OK?! I don't like this place and all these people repeating "Hare Krishna" all the time' was his answer.

When I went to the cowshed, I saw Milena talking with Logan. He was explaining the work to her.

'Hey, Albanian, grab a pitchfork and clean the shit,' said Logan in his evil way.

'Hey, Logan! I have a name: Martin!'

I was a bit angry with Logan, just because of his jealousy. Since Milena saw me, she approached and suggested we take some pictures. It is funny how much people like photos, as they want to take them even inside a dirty shed! She was playing topless in between the bulls and cows, but being self-conscious, of course, she was laughing while doing it.

After finishing our work and the photos, we went to the castle. Just before we arrived, Niki ran up to us, crying. She directly embraced Milena and couldn't stop crying.

'What's wrong, Niki?! Why are you crying?' asked Milena.

'Josh and Manuel were beating each other! Oh, it was horrible! I'm not used to seeing these kinds of scenes.'

I saw a bunch of people behind the castle, including Manuel, holding his jaw with a paper towel turning red from the bleeding. Josh had already disappeared already. I didn't want to ask Manuel what had happened. Zolla, another volunteer, explained to us that everything that happened was because Manuel wasn't working as hard as the other volunteers, and his answer to Josh had been 'You are a doll here!' Josh's response had been to straight away punch Manuel in the jaw.

I knew Josh was well trained, as he'd worked as a security guard in the same company as Logan.

Harvey came along, not caring about the situation. He advised us to continue with the work in the garden.

Kai and Simon came a bit later. All we had to do was finish the hugelkultur bed we'd started the day before. In two hours the hugelkultur bed was done. We left the tools and lay down in the garden, sleeping like the dead. The rest didn't last even five minutes.

Harvey appeared again, shouting, 'Hey! What are you doing, sleeping in the garden?! I asked you to work, not to sleep!'

'We just finished what was supposed to be done, Harvey,' I retorted.

'There's always something to do here! Come on, stand up! Start with another hugelkultur bed,' Harvey ordered.

Lunchtime wasn't far off, and to start digging a new trench was a nightmare for all of us. Sometimes people abuse volunteers in work exchange. Maybe they see volunteers as work animals. If you work like a donkey, they're gonna make you work like a horse; if you work like a horse, they're gonna laugh at you. Respect just those few hours of volunteer work, and that's it—that's why it is called 'work exchange', volunteer work with no pay; it is supposed to be fun as well. We took the tools, but we didn't do any work; we just waited for lunchtime. We sat outside on the veranda, as the sun was shining like it did in springtime. All the volunteers were sitting at one table. I saw that Logan took a place close to Milena. I shouldn't be jealous. She wasn't my girlfriend, even though I'd already sent her a message via Facebook saying that I liked her lips. This was supposed to be romantic, even though I liked her breasts more.

That afternoon, the work in the garden got more boring, as Simon didn't stop complaining about everything, not even for one second.

'Creepy castle!' he said 'I shouldn't have come here. Look at all these psychopaths around! I'm gonna ask you a favour, guys. I want to go to the woods tonight; please join me. I need some peace, a quiet space where I can breathe freely. I have had enough of hearing all these theories. This is not normal; I can't accept it!'

After dinner, we all joined Simon, apart from Manuel, who was busy packing all his stuff to leave the next morning. Simon brought his portable stereo along. It was dark, and we all had lighters on. Going through the woods during the night was a bit awkward, avoiding slushy potholes and slipping on the sloping ground. Simon did put some music on his stereo, but when we got to the top of the hill, he switched to a priest talking about Jesus for half an hour. For me, Jesus and Hare Krishna were the same: just philosophy, knowledge, and culture. I have no religion! I believe in what I see and what I feel; it can be any kind of believing, religious or not. It's personal, and I don't judge people for being part of any kind of religion!

Anyway, I enjoyed eating the sweet chocolate Simon gave us, and I sat close to Milena, which I enjoyed even more. She put her head on my shoulder, and we watched the stars. For me, the priest became a poet, the most romantic singer, and this night became special. Why? Because Milena lifted her head, and I didn't hesitate to kiss her. I didn't want to wait any more, and it was the perfect occasion. I could feel her dry lips on mine. No one was watching. At least that was what I thought in that moment. It didn't last even five seconds. When I wanted to slide my tongue into her mouth, she stopped.

The next day, Manuel and Kai both left. Simon took a day off, and I had to work alone with Logan in the garden. I saw Vade from Holland playing his harmonica on the other side of the garden, but he left directly when he saw Logan.

I felt a bit uncomfortable, just because Logan also liked Milena, and I had exchanged my first kiss with her the night before. Nonetheless, this didn't prevent me from talking freely, as I always did.

'For how long are you planning to stay, Martin? Do you want to continue as a volunteer, or are you going to try something else and make some money?' asked Logan.

'For the moment, I'm staying here, as they need always someone. I don't think I can find a better place than this one right now. I like the food, and I have good company. It doesn't bother me if I hear the same words, "Hare Krishna", all day, and all these people talking about it. It doesn't even bother me to hear Vade's alarm; I'm getting used to switching it off each morning.'

'Ha ha! I can't deal with that guy any more. Why don't you kick him when his alarm goes off? That's what I do.'

'I'm not used to kicking people, Logan. But, someday, I'm gonna break his smartphone,' I said, laughing. 'And what about your plans? Are you moving somewhere else as a volunteer, or are you looking for a paying job?'

'I'm not sure I can be easily accepted via Work Exchange because I don't have any comments on my profile. But I'll figure out in a few days if I have to find a real job. Why not make some real money?!'

'Well, you can join me for the bank robbery if you want the real thing,' I said, joking.

'Take it easy—'

He let his voice trail off, but I heard him say, 'fucking Albanian'; it was difficult to catch it, maybe because he didn't want me to hear it. I heard it, though, but I didn't say anything.

After lunch, I went to relax in the reception area, reading the book Dimitri had given me, *The Journey of Self-Discovery*. The book was an interview of a member of the Hare Krishna religion, explaining facts about spiritual life. The first example consisted of the inviolability of mind and spirit. As the body grows in time, our experiences expand further, but we remain the same. The second example was more interesting, comparing body and soul with a car and a driver. I read just a few pages, and I left.

On the second floor, I found Vade's harmonica on the floor near a big vase. When I went up to the dormitory, I saw Logan.

'Hey, did you just become a musician? That's Vade's harmonica, right?' asked Logan.

'Yes, I found it downstairs. I'm just waiting to see him so I can give it back to him. I couldn't leave it there; someone else could steal it,' I said.

After five minutes, Vade came in, and I didn't hesitate to give him back his instrument.

'Thank you!' he said. 'You are a good boy, Albanian; I totally forgot where I left it. I owe you!'

'Well, if you want to return the favour, Vade, maybe you have an extra pair of headphones I could have, as mine are broken.'

Logan gave me a sideways glance, and then he left the room.

I was being a bit of a smart alec, but I didn't have any negative purpose. Vade gave me a pair of headphones, and I was excited to hear my favourite songs once again.

At nine o'clock, my stomach started to make noise. I went to the castle to get some food. Milena and Niki joined me. There was no food left in the kitchen. Mourad passed through the corridor, and I asked him if he could get us some food. In his kind and helpful way Mourad came back with two baskets. He joined us and began to talk about religion and Krishna's love.

'You know, Mourad, I respect your feelings about your god, Krishna, but I believe that God is everywhere, in everything positive.'

'I respect your belief as well, Martin. However, the way you believe in God is impersonal. Many people have many gods, but there's just one true God.'

'I also believe that love for someone else—a partner or a spouse—can be the highest form of pure and positive energy,' I said.

At that moment Niki, laughed and said something to Milena.

'What you just said is a mirror of loving God, the true eternal!' said Mourad 'I have been married twice, but the happiness each of my wives gave me only lasted for a short time. I was rich before, but I couldn't find real happiness by spending money. Not too long ago, I heard about a billionaire businessman who killed himself because he lost almost everything. Afterwards, they discovered that he had still five million dollars in his bank account. Here, I'm happy, Martin. I wake up at five in the morning, I take a shower, and I go to the temple to join the others. We start the day with dancing and singing in front of the gods. This is what makes me happy.'

The discussion lasted long enough to end with my stomach full, and I was very grateful to Mourad. I noticed that Milena and Niki weren't interested in hearing his philosophy, but I was. It didn't influence my own beliefs, but I accept his views and appreciated his knowledge.

On the way back to the guest house, Niki went to the library, as it was open till late at night.

I was alone with Milena. When we arrived in front the room where she and Niki slept, Milena opened the door.

I asked, 'Can I come in?'

'Sorry, Martin. I think you are rushing things a little bit. I like you, but … I don't feel it!'

I was a bit sad but not disappointed; I had even expected this response. I just wanted to profit from any occasion, as the time I had at the castle was limited, and I didn't want to lose any chance to be with Milena.

The next day, I discovered that Milena's reaction was a sign of something entirely different to what I initially thought.

Just after I finished breakfast, Harvey called out to me, telling me to follow him. He was very quiet as he led me outside to the veranda. I saw Baghavati and Logan sitting at the first table. A strange feeling permeated my body. Harvey pulled up a chair joined them, and I was left to stand in front of them.

Baghavati spoke first, saying, 'Martin, I really appreciate your hard work and the help you provide to us, but I can't accept that a volunteer would steal something from someone else! I'm really disappointed in what you did with Vade. Logan explained to me everything that happened yesterday.'

At that moment, Logan bowed his head.

'Don't look at Logan or pretend he is to blame!' said Baghavati. 'He has spent a long time here; after Harvey, he's the one responsible for everything that happens in the guest house. I feel sorry that a volunteer with a good attitude like yours could do something like this. This is not acceptable! Whenever we hear that something has been stolen, we call the police immediately!'

The strange feeling permeating my body start to tease my anger. This was just Logan's plan to get me into trouble.

'Hey!' I said. 'If someone else here has stolen something, then I can't be the first to do it. I didn't steal Vade's harmonica. I found it, and I brought it to the dormitory to give it back to him. That doesn't mean that I stole it, OK?!'

'After you gave it back, Martin, what did you do? You asked Vade to return the favour. In this religion it is prohibited to ask someone to return a favour. What were you thinking when you found Vade's harmonica? That you could profit from returning it, maybe?' asked Logan, lifting up his head to show his yellow teeth and the evil shining in his eyes.

'I—'

Baghavati interrupted me, saying, 'Logan is right. Our religion strictly prohibits anyone from asking for the return of a favour.'

'Sorry,' I said. 'But wait a minute. Who said that I'm part of your religion? Maybe I forgot to say that I'm an atheist, even I have always respected your rules. I'm not part of Hare Krishna like you are. Logan may say he's feeling sorry for Vade now, but he totally forgot what he suggested to me before: to kick him instead of switching off the alarm on his mobile!'

'Well … yes, I said to kick him,' Logan said. 'But I meant to wake up him! Just a small kick; hardly a kick at all really.'

I thought Logan would have nothing left to say to justify himself now, but, of course, his evil plan was well designed, and he manipulated it to last longer.

'Martin! Can you tell us once more about your plan to rob a bank? Do you think that an Albanian like you can be a good example for the other volunteers?' asked Logan.

'OK, that's enough!' said Baghavati. 'I think this discussion should end right now! If I have something more to say, Martin, I know where to find you. For the moment, I suggest you join the other volunteers and forget about any consequences.'

With that, Baghavati left.

Logan had used things I'd said and done to concoct a story to tell Baghavati, just to make trouble for me. It was all because of jealousy.

The days passed quickly. After that brief kiss, nothing happened with Milena. She started to be colder towards me for no reason. One evening, as I walked to the dormitory, I saw Logan and Milena.

Milena pushed him, saying, 'Stop touching me, Logan! Leave me alone!'

I excused myself as I passed between them. I didn't want to say anything to Logan. He stopped when Milena told him to, which was good, because I couldn't have stopped him and then justified my actions as her boyfriend. It was just a kiss, and saying or doing anything with Logan now could be a mistake—especially in front of Milena.

The work in the garden became even more boring. Simon now complained all the time, never stopping.

Suddenly Josh appeared again, and the situation changed. He had been staying with friends in

Brussels, and he had to get Baghavati's permission to return to the castle. Josh was surprised because Baghavati not only accepted his request but also offered him a private sleeping room in another building. True, Josh had defended the rules of volunteers' duties and behaviour, which Manuel hadn't respected at all, but Josh had still committed an act of violence.

I explained to Josh the current situation with Logan, glad that now I had a better company than before. As Simon was only a teenager, I couldn't share everything with him, but Josh was someone I could accept advice from.

We were sitting in our usual room, I told Josh something about my difficult past.

He looked at me and said, 'Look, Martin, you are not the only one coming from a ruined past. All the people you see here are the same. You don't have any idea how much I suffer because I left my family behind. I started to travel, just to find some peace, even though it's almost impossible for me because I have a daughter who's gonna be in a wheelchair for the rest of her life. She will never get married. It's not that she's ... I mean, she's smart and understands everything, but she's paralysed. I left everything I had to my wife and my daughter. I'm divorced now.'

I couldn't say anything to comfort him. I just felt so sad to hear what he had just told me.

With that, he stood up and said, 'Come on, mate, no worries. Let's take something left in the kitchen.'

We'd just found some sweets when a lady all covered with a mantle shouted, 'Don't eat standing up! If you do, you could be a horse in your next life!'

I didn't say anything. Josh just laughed.

She was a devotee, and, of course, their beliefs included reincarnation. They also believed that if you killed a cow, you would reincarnate as a cow; they believed the same about killing any kind of animal, and even cutting trees.

When I went back to the dormitory, a bad smell teased my nose. Someone wearing dirty, torn clothes lay on the left side of the room. It was even weirder when I noticed that no one was around him. Mourad explained to me that the man had returned to the castle for a second time, coming from a psychiatric hospital. He became a nightmare for all of us in the dormitory, with that bad smell. The windows were open, but opened them wider. This was just the start of what would happen later.

I took the next day off. I planned to visit Durbuy, the closest town, just a four-kilometre walk. It was the smallest town in the world, with fewer than ten thousand inhabitants. The town was elevated to the rank of city in 1331 by John I, the king of Bohemia. Niki accompanied me to Durbuy. Unfortunately, I couldn't have Milena's company. When I asked her to join me, she justified her refusal by saying that she had already taken a day off the weekend before. I didn't understand her cold attitude, but as we walked, Niki explained to me that Milena wasn't too satisfied with the community, her first experience doing a work exchange.

That evening, I met the other guys in the kitchen. They were discussing the new problem: the bad smell. Vade's alarm was nothing in comparison.

'We should talk to Baghavati about this problem. Maybe she can give us a solution,' suggested Logan.

'The only solution here, Logan, is to kick him out; but we can't do that because Mr Bad Smell paid ten euros to stay here. I don't have even the slightest idea where he got it. We just have to wait till he leaves. Last year, he was only here for ten days,' said Harvey.

'Ten days?! I have to find another room, and I'm ready to pay for it!' said Simon.

At that moment, Mr Bad Smell appeared from nowhere and stood in front of us. I noticed that Simon's mouth was open. No one spoke or moved. Now I could see the man very clearly: he had grey eyes and an ugly, rotten face covered with wrinkles. He looked to be around 50 to 60 years old. He wore a Russian hat and a torn coat. As big as a bear, he was the creepiest men I had ever seen. He grabbed a plate and took some food from the baskets, using his hands. There was a deep silence. After he left, I saw that Simon closed his mouth.

Josh broke the silence, saying, 'Who want to take some food now?!'

No one was hungry any more. We all left the kitchen and went to the dormitory. Fortunately, that night the creepy man wasn't there. Josh joined us in the dormitory as well.

When I asked him why, he just threw a sideways glance at Logan and said, 'People talk!'

The next morning, when we asked Harvey if Mr Bad Smell had left, he said, 'No! He slept in the garden!'

At half past three that afternoon, Simon and I were in our secret room. He was telling me about his plans to visit Amsterdam. I couldn't join him, as I only had enough money to pay for a train ticket to my next destination.

At that moment, we heard someone whispering in the corridor, repeating the same words over and over. This time, it was not 'Hare Krishna', but someone saying, 'I want to kill people. I want to kill people.'

I went to check and saw someone moving through the corridor with an axe over his shoulder.

I noticed that Simon had open his mouth like a grave this time. He said, 'Don't tell me! It's Mr Bad Smell, isn't it?'

I didn't answer.

'This is insane!' screamed Simon.

After our last duty that evening, Harvey was waiting for us in the kitchen.

'I heard about what happened, guys!' Harvey said. 'Whatever he does or says, I advise you to just ignore him; just stay away. Last time, he didn't do anything bad. I know that he was in a psychiatric hospital for a long time, but I can't call the police just for the bad-smell reason.'

When I went back to the guest house, I saw Milena playing with her tablet as I reached the second floor. I sat next to her, and I asked about her current situation and if she was planning to move somewhere else. I chose my words carefully and spoke in a low voice. I was surprised me when she told me that she had still two weeks to spend in this community. The discussion became more interesting when she began to talk about her family and her prior life. She was talking and talking, and I just stared without saying a word. I looked at her big brown eyes, her tiny nose, and her thick lips. This time, I didn't kiss her; I wasn't in the right position as she put her head back on the chair. The discussion ended with a goodnight and a smile.

Fortunately, Mr Bad Smell wasn't in the dormitory that night, and so I had a deep sleep.

I held an Albanian flag. It fluttered in the breeze—a black double-headed eagle surrounded by red. I wasn't smiling or showing any sign of joy or pride. At that moment, I felt something approach me. From far away, it was just a black thing becoming bigger and bigger. Now, it was just a few metres away, and I could see the shape of a man, but it was difficult to see his face. It wasn't a human being but a ghost, standing in front of me and not doing anything.

Then, I heard someone scream, '*Ru-u-u-u-u-u-un!*'

I turned my head and saw Simon's face covered in blood.

I woke up. It was just a dream, a nightmare. I saw a ghost right in front of me, and I didn't even believe in ghosts. Sometimes dreams could be really sophisticated. It then became difficult to distinguish what was real from what was not real. But the feeling of trepidation I felt upon waking up was real.

I looked at the clock; it was almost half past three. I felt a sleep again.

A shrill noise pierced my ears. I started to open my eyes, but it was difficult to wake up. I was still tired from the poor night's sleep. Finally, I managed to keep my eyes open. I saw someone going through the dormitory, pulling an axe.

It was Mr Bad Smell, whispering the same words Simon and I had heard the day before: 'I want to kill people. I want to kill people. I want to kill people.'

I dared not peek to see what he was doing. This time, I was really afraid and it wasn't because of a dream. The nightmare was becoming reality.

The whole thing only lasted three minutes, and then he left. Nothing happened.

It was a quarter past eight in the morning, and everyone was usually awake by that time.

Then, someone said, 'No one has to be afraid, guys. I was here last year when he arrived, and I think this is just his habit—nothing more.'

That was the weirdest habit I had ever seen or heard! It became even weirder when I discovered that the reception staff never tried to change the entrance password.

After breakfast, we began with the daily tasks.

Simon had taken already a room apart and paid for it.

I was sitting alone in front of the castle, and Milena came to join me. We were talking and laughing. After a while, we went for a walk outside the castle. I felt like the happiest guy in the world.

For a moment, she changed the subject, saying, 'Hey, Martin, I heard about what happened between you and Logan! Niki told me. He invited me to see Amsterdam, but after hearing all this, I just cancelled.'

I didn't say anything; I just smiled.

Mr Bad Smell kept walking through the corridors, repeating the same words, and it became a usual thing. It was just his habit, and no one was afraid any more.

One evening, I was sitting in the kitchen with Simon, Josh, and Logan, and we heard a voice say, 'I want to kill people.'

After five seconds of silence, everyone was laughing.

Josh grabbed an empty plastic glass from the garbage and threw it straight at Mr Bad Smell.

'Go kill yourself, you crazy fuck!' shouted Josh.

The glass flew through the air and touched the back of his shoulder. Mr Bad Smell stopped for a second and then started to walk again at a brisk pace.

'Hey, Josh! What are you doing, mate? You shouldn't! Harvey told us not to do anything. Did you forget?' shouted Logan.

'I can't support someone talking shit all time as he does, mate! Someone has to do something. Someone has to kick him out!' screamed Josh with anger.

'And you think throwing a plastic glass at him is the solution? Whatever! I'm not responsible for whatever might happen. I stayed here for one year, and it was easy just to respect the rules,' said Logan, this time in a lower voice.

We left the kitchen without saying any more. I went to the dormitory and lay down. I felt so tired.

The next morning, I woke up later than usual. I went to brush my teeth and stopped moving for a moment. It felt like my heart was beating slower than normal. I tried to breathe deeply for a few minutes.

When I reached the castle, breakfast had already been served. Fortunately, I found some warm porridge left in the kitchen. I finished it in five minutes, and then I ran outside, where met Josh.

'Hey, Josh! How you doing? Do you know where the others are?' I asked.

'I don't know, Martin. I just got here, and I didn't eat breakfast either. It's my day off, so don't look so surprised,' he said.

It was a perfect sunny day to take off. I should do the same, but I had to ask Harvey for permission. I went to the reception area to ask for him, as that was the easiest way to find someone without looking too much, and there I found Baghavati. I asked her for the day off, and her answer was yes, along with a big smile. Even after that incident with Logan, she never changed her positive attitude towards me; I think maybe she knew that I wasn't actually guilty.

Now that I had the day off, I started to think about what I should with my free time. My first thought was to go back to the dormitory, listen to some music, read something, or even just lie down and enjoy the silence. A day off should be exactly that: time off, without doing anything. I started to listen to some of my favourite hits, and then I fell asleep for a few hours.

When I woke up, I felt more tired than before. Something strange was happening to me. I had a headache that I couldn't get rid of. When I went outside, clouds covered the sun, and the sky was transformed from blue to dark grey. I was in front of the dining area when I heard someone screaming. Then, there were more screams! My heart started to beat faster. Something was happening. I didn't see anyone in front of the castle. Whatever was happening must be going on at the rear of the castle. Then, I a saw a monk running. I started to run as well. Someone was screaming in pain.

I reached the grounds behind the castle. There were so many people. All those terrified faces! I made my way through the crowd, and I saw Logan covered in blood—he wasn't the one screaming. It was Josh! His right arm was cut and hanging by just a thread of flesh. Josh just kept screaming.

I started to feel weak; I couldn't feel my body any more! I wished this could be just a nightmare, but I knew it was real.

I saw Martin standing in front of that scene! It was foggy and hard to see. I didn't understand what was happening to me. I was watching myself! Then, I saw Milena. There was a terrified expression on her face, and her big eyes were filled with tears. I watched myself walk straight to her.

Simon stood just beside Milena. To say he was scared was not sufficient to describe the look on his pale face.

'What happened?' I asked.

No answer. Milena was frozen and couldn't say a word.

'What happened, Simon?!' I asked.

'I just got here, Martin. But I can imagine who did this,' answered Simon, his lips trembling. He bowed his head and started crying.

I could still hear Josh screaming in pain, and my heart broke just thinking about his life now. His life? What about his family? His daughter?

Logan tied an old T-shirt around Josh's arm, just above the cut, to stop the bleeding. In that moment, Logan was a hero to me, as I couldn't do any better.

After a few minutes, I heard sirens. I didn't want to be interrogated or even checked by any cops.

The best move for me now was to run away. It was not smart for illegals to participate in this kind of scenario. When I reached the dormitory, I thought the cops might come here to investigate. The best thing for me was to run away from this place. Why not take a long walk and go far from the castle?

I walked for four hours—heartbroken and tired. I began thinking about leaving soon as possible. When I got back to the guest house, I saw Logan with a bunch of people around him. He was explaining what had happened. I wasn't curious to hear anything for the moment. I was tired, and the first thing I wanted to do was to visit the Work Exchange site to search for another host.

As I walked through the corridor, Milena came out of her room.

'Hey, Martin! It's good to see you. Come here; I want to hug you. This was too much for me; I can't afford to be alone now. Niki left an hour ago. She went to Brussels to stay with her friend. I'm leaving tomorrow! I just booked a flight to Portugal; that will be easier for me, as I'm not fluent in English. I miss my language.'

'Good for you!' were the only words I could express in that moment.

My heart started beating faster. It was difficult to breathe. She was watching me, and what I read in her eyes was *I want you, Martin; I'm all yours now! Come and fuck me!*

But what she said was 'I'm gonna miss you, Martin!'

I grabbed her by the waist. A blast of energy and desire started to explode inside me. I was kissing her, touching her body, feeling her soft breasts against my chest, and going slowly into her room. I took off my shoes while kissing her, while touching her. It was a feeling I'd never felt before, as this was the first time. Everything surrounding us vanished in the moment. I took off her clothes one by one, and we lay down on that messy bed. I kissed her neck, her big, soft breasts, and then down and down. I penetrated her body, and I heard her groaning and groaning. My body was on fire, and she was screaming from desire. She became red, and I became all pink.

I accompanied her to the train station the next morning; she was taking the train to the airport. We just hugged goodbye without kissing.

When I got back, I met Simon and Logan in the garden.

'What happened yesterday?' I asked Logan.

'When I got there, that bastard had already left. Dimitri was there from at the beginning and saw everything. He said it was the first time he ever heard that man talking normally, even loudly, but Josh didn't say a word. You know it was his habit to punch people instead of saying something. Unfortunately, he didn't put down that freaking giant, and his countering was what you saw yourself.'

'Do you know anything about Josh's current condition?' I asked.

'Well, he's missing an arm now, but he will survive. Are you really worried about his health, Martin? Fucking that Brazilian girl on the same day it happened, I don't think you were too worried, were you?'

I didn't answer.

'Hey, come on, Martin, everyone passing that door could hear Milena's groans.'

Simon was laughing and said, 'I could do the same if my grandma died!'

I didn't expect this kind of answer from him, knowing his faith, but I took it as a teenager's version of support.

I grabbed a shovel and I joined them to finish the work they had already started.

During lunchtime I was sitting alone on the couch in the big hall inside the castle. Two monks came and joined me. As I was sitting in the middle, one monk sat on the left side, and the other one on the right. The monk on the left was looked Indian, with a mole in between his eyes. Curious, I asked about it.

'This is one reason that I make a fake mole on my forehead,' said. 'As I'm part of this religion, I want to explain people who don't know about it; I mean to people who don't share our beliefs. It's the third eye; meaning, the gate which leads to the inner realms of higher consciousness—on this case to Krishna consciousness. It is the power of imagination and understanding. Our real eyes can only show us what's physical, but what you believe and understand comes from the third eye.'

'In what do you believe? What's your perception of life?' I asked, remembering my questions before leaving my country.

'I believe in what I see and what I feel, but more in what I feel than what I see,' he replied. 'Sometimes we need to make big changes in our lives and renounce everything in order to start a new path which leads to the truth. In that moment we choose karma. The Bhagvad Gita says that at a certain point in our lives, when we are afraid, we ask the greatest of all, the universe, and we receive an answer.'

'You didn't answer the second question the young man asked,' said the monk on the right. 'What's life, young man? 'Life is a dream.'

'If I believe that, then I have to be a passive sleepwalker!' I said sarcastically.

'Or an active dream walker,' replied the monk. 'You know, I have a daughter, and I love her, but I'm conscious that this is not true. What you see around you is just a dream. It's a lie.'

The days became suddenly colder. When Simon left, I had to stay alone most of time. I had to shave my head, as I didn't have much money left, and kept my head covered with a hat all the time. I sent an email to Sint Lucas Monastery, as Charlie and Mia suggested I do in Luxembourg. I got an answer next day, and I had two days to get ready for the next adventure. It was the right time to change places in those winter days, since it was almost impossible to do even the easiest jobs in the garden.

Harvey accompanied me to the train station.

After we shook hands, he said, 'Thanks for all your help, Martin; I hope to see you again!'

As I put my suitcase in the train car, he almost screamed above the train whistle, 'And bring back that Range Rover, Martin! Remember that our brain is the lamp of Aladdin. Make a wish.'

Remembering his funny face kept my good sense of humour during my trip to Niest station. After that experience in the Krishna community, answers questions and answers arose inside me.

Why was the universe created? It's a universal question, but everything in the universe is relative. I started to see my life as a mission, that I was born to do something. When I thought back to my special dream with the pink boy, I saw that I was telling myself that it was a dream to show me not to be afraid. The Krishna theory said the same about life.

And what about God's love? Mourad said that love for someone else was a mirror of loving God, but God was inside us and we ourselves are God—and that love is and should remain eternal.

4

THE LONG WAY TO NORWAY

In the bike parking lot I found a telephone booth. Stella answered. She was in charge of the monastery. I had to wait just fifteen minutes, and someone came to pick me up. He was called Zac and appeared to be around 60 years old. The monastery was just a ten-minute drive away, and Zac wasn't driving even fast. From the main road, we turned right, drove along a straight, long path, and ended up in front of a large building. At the right of the entrance, Zac showed me his workshop, which he called 'his laboratory'.

After going to the second floor, I entered the room I was going to stay in for a few weeks. I set my suitcase in the corner, and Zac waited to show me the rest of the building. It became the biggest I had ever stayed in, almost three times bigger than the Krishna castle. From the windows I could see the backyard.

We walked through the long corridor and stopped at the last door on the left, entering the community kitchen. It was half past six, and everyone was waiting for me. The soup had already been served, and the bowls were on the table. I introduced myself, and everyone told me their names while remaining in their seats. The only one who stood up to shake my hand was Stella. A cute blonde around 30 years old. Her husband came five minutes later. He was also called Martin. A tall well-dressed man with long hair. He held his son in his arms, a two-year-old called Leon.

Everyone complimented the soup.

Suddenly Stella asked, 'For how long do you want to stay with us, Martin?'

'For a few weeks, maybe just a few days more than that,' I said.

'That is a short stay!' she said. 'However, you can stay as long as you want. For the moment, you are the only volunteer. In a few weeks another volunteer, a girl from Germany, will join us for a stay of six months.'

I had already made a plan for my trip to Scandinavia. Before passing through Germany, I didn't want to miss the chance to see Amsterdam; that was why I couldn't be precise about my departure date just yet.

'One last question, Martin,' continued Stella. 'Why do you wear a hat? It's so warm in here! You can take it off.'

'Sorry, Stella, but I can't. I would feel very uncomfortable without it, as I'd look like a prisoner,' I answered.

'I'm really curious to see what you look like without it,' continued Stella. 'Maybe I'll have to come to your room while you're asleep and take it off.'

I didn't expect this kind of answer. My face and ears were burning. Her husband was right there, listening.

After a long discussion, I understood the position of each one in that community.

The organizer was Jossif, a short man with a beard. He looked like an amateur priest, but he was actually just an ordinary person practising his philosophies.

Katherine immediately became my best friend there. A fat, round girl, very nice and cosy, ready to listen to all my stories.

After dinner, I went to my room to unpack everything from my suitcase. I lay down on the bed and didn't wait long to fall asleep.

The next morning, I woke to the sound of loud music. I dressed quickly and went down to the interior hall, which was where the sound of the music came from. People were dancing in the hallway! Stella came and grabbed me. She was dancing and smiling, and I started to do the same thing, without having even the slightest idea of what was going on. It lasted for just a few minutes, and then someone switched off the stereo.

'This is the way we wake up, Martin,' Stella explained. 'We split the duties for today, so you're gonna start by helping in the kitchen. Afterwards, my husband needs you to move some heavy stuff in the restaurant.'

In the kitchen I met a Spanish guy a bit younger than me. I started calling him *el Cuthinero*. We were speaking in Spanish, and all I had to do was cut some vegetables. After I finished in the kitchen, I sat in the restaurant, waiting for Stella's husband, Martin.

I waited for fifteen minutes and suddenly heard someone whispering at the entrance.

'Sorry, I'm talking to myself!' said Martin.

'No worries! I do that also,' I said. I didn't, not even sometimes, but I said it to comfort him.

Martin wanted me to put up some cupboards. They were quite heavy, and he got Zac to help me.

When the bell rang, lunch was already served on the table outside on the veranda. About twenty of us sat around the table. The food was mostly vegetarian, but it couldn't compare with the food at the Krishna community. As my stay was likely going to be short, I never complained. The leftovers were covered with plastic, put back in the fridge, and ready to be served again the next day.

I had a break till four o'clock, and then I would go back into the kitchen to finish with the dishwashing.

I was resting in my room when Katherine came by and suggested we go for a walk. I started telling her about my trip to Norway, explaining that I hoped to earn some money there.

'Do not worry too much about money, Martin; the day will come for you too. I'm gonna tell you something personal about that, but please do not share it with anyone.'

'OK.'

'After becoming a nurse, it was difficult for me to find a job. When I finally found one, the salary wasn't enough for me to meet my expenses. Afterwards, I got some new connections through my boyfriend. It was actually a mafia organization. I was still a nurse, but I earned much more money than I had before. I quit a long time ago, and the money still comes to me.'

'How?!' I asked, curious to discover how such an arrangement worked.

'You are not the only one to ask me this question. A lot of friends ask me the same thing when I buy an expensive laptop or take a holiday wherever I want. I just bought an ugly car because I don't want to show off too much. I want to keep myself away from troubles. Even here people can be very greedy for fancy stuff. Now I'm planning to find a place where I can spend my future.'

'With some lucky man, eh?!'

'Who, Jossif?' Katherine said with a laugh.

'What?!' I was surprised, as I thought that Jossif was just an amateur priest.

'Yes, Martin. This is another secret that I'm sharing with you. I love him. Ever since we first met, I thought he should definitely be my husband.'

'I'm happy for you Katherine!'

I could share everything with Katherine, and we spent most of our free time together. Sometimes I visited her in her room, the biggest and most comfortable one there.

I started a new job in the garden, putting mulch around the flowers and trees. First, I had to put some cardboard, as Jossif advised me, so that the mulch would last longer. He had to go away for a few days, and Stella had to choose someone else to be the organizer.

Stella told me that this huge property had been purchased for five million euros by a large group of people (herself and 120 others, some of whom also lived there). They received income from the restaurant and room rentals, as some of the big rooms were often rented for meetings and special events. She explained that this income wasn't as much as predicted, and they were planning to sell the property.

Stella had to leave the monastery for two days, and Martin asked if I could take care of their son for half a day. I didn't have any idea how take care of kids, as I never been close to them, and now I had to work as their babysitter.

'What am I supposed to do?' I asked Martin.

'It's easy,' he said. 'You just have to follow him around and play with him.'

He was right. Leon was easy to take care of, playing and laughing all the time. When Stella came back, I took the weekend off.

On Monday, I joined Tom, Jossif's replacement. Tom was an electrician, and all I had to do was pull some wires in the attic. It was a new arrangement for increasing the Internet speed by 200 per cent. As Tom was an expert in connections, he set new rules about Internet use. After midnight, the Internet had to be disabled, as there was a good chance the interference of the router could disturb our mental health. I had never heard that before, but when I thought about how everyone had a mobile or smartphone on all the time, there would be interference constantly. I wasn't worried about it, and I didn't share my opinion, especially since I usually slept later than noon.

I had already started to plan my trip to Scandinavia. Since I didn't want to miss the chance of seeing Amsterdam, I sent an email to the Dutch family I'd met in southern France. I wasn't surprised when they agreed to have me stay, as they had already invited me to visit.

The last days in the monastery turned into a tragedy for Katherine. I saw her going out of the kitchen, crying and slamming the door. After five minutes of thinking about whether to follow her, I decided to knock on her door, to give her a hug and wait to hear about the bad news she must have just received.

When I knocked, she opened the door, saying, 'I loved him, and I was ready to give everything I had.'

'I feel really sorry for you, Katherine,' I said, trying to console her, as I immediately understood that she and Jossif had broken up.

Jossif cheated on her—with a man. He was definitely gay. Katherine explained to me that he was gay before they met each other.

When I went out of Katherine's room, I met Stella in the corridor.

She was smiling and said, 'It is so nice that you stay close to Katherine these days, Martin.'

'Yes, I know she needs a friend now. At least I can be there for her for three days I have left to be here.'

'Ah, for a moment I forgot about your short stay.'

Five seconds after I walked past her, Stella called, 'Martin, wait! I have to tell you something. Tonight, we are organizing a special event for forty people. They're gonna eat dinner in our restaurant, and I need you to serve them some drinks after midnight. I mean, it's not just a simple dinner but more like a party. I would like you to join us if you want to see something special.'

Her last words felt a bit provocative; I mean, there was something about her smile. *Something special,* I thought.

I was serving beers, and exactly at midnight the lights were switched off. A half-naked stripper put on a show, dancing on the tables, showing off her big fake boobs. Her final move was unforgivable. She put her legs up in the air and inserted a firework fake penis into her vagina. I heard screams and loud music, and smoke filled the room. Fire alarms started to sound, and that became a sign to end the show.

I stayed late night to finish with the dishwashing. Everyone had left, and I still ten glasses to wash.

'Hey, Martin! Did you enjoy the show?'

I turned to see Stella.

'Heh heh. Yes, of course, I enjoyed it!' I lied.

'You can finish with the glasses and then come help me put the bottles back in the refrigerator room,' she said.

'Yes, of course,' I answered, a bit nervous.

I followed her to the refrigerator room, and suddenly she turned and stood in front of me, just staring at me. There was no time for me to say even a word. The best thing was to grab her ass and give her what she wanted. And I did. It didn't last even five minutes. After that first time with Milena, I never thought I could have such a quick sex. But that was it; no one had to know, especially not in my last two days there.

I found someone via BlaBlaCar to take me from Brussels to Amsterdam.

Katherine accompanied me to the train station. I gave her one last hug and then boarded the train straight to Brussels. I had to wait half an hour for the driver to pick me up. As I was in the Schengen area, I wasn't too worried about the borders. I enjoyed the trip, listening my favourites, and halfway there I fell asleep. When he stopped the car, I opened my eyes to see that we had arrived at my destination.

The generous family was waiting for me in Amsterdam, where I spent four beautiful days. One day, I spent all my time visiting the famous monuments and museums, which I really enjoyed. It was easy just to follow the long boulevard and pass through Dam Square, Van Gogh Museum, Vondelpark, and so on. Amsterdam is known as the Northern Venice, and the way I travelled through it made it become the most interesting city. I didn't smoke weed or go to a nightclub, as I really should have done to get to know the real spirit of this glamorous city. I had just enough money for my ticket to Hamburg. It was difficult to find the best words to describe how grateful I was to this family, but I decided to let the future decide the way I would express my gratitude.

After arriving at the Hamburg train station, I had just some coins left, and I wasn't sure if it was enough for a bus ticket to reach my destination. I could try hitch-hiking, as the village was just an hour away.

I asked the bus driver about the ticket price, and I was ready to leave when he told me.

He understood my problem and said, 'Come in, young man. Give me what you have, and I'll give you a ticket; but do not say anything to the next driver, as you will have to change buses after three stations.'

I just smiled and said, 'Thank you.'

I had met so many people ready to help me, even though they didn't really know me. Sometimes I felt so happy that it became difficult to believe that all this was real. *Is it a dream?* I often wondered. For me, it was both real and a dream, and it became part of my emotions, a beautiful feeling which accompanied throughout my entire journey.

My next host was called Merle. It wasn't difficult to find Merle's house; I had asked the kind bus driver and then just followed his directions. After walking on a long path, I ended up at a huge farmhouse. I saw a boy playing outside. This must be the son Merle had mentioned. He was not more than 10 years old but very polite, kindly introducing himself, even though his English was poor. We went inside the house, and I saw a big living room, which included the kitchen, a library, a modern fireplace, and a long dining table. Merle came home later, and the whole family sat around the table at dinner time.

Since it was my first night there, I didn't hesitate to share my story. New hosts always wanted to know about their volunteers. I introduced myself as Martin the Pink Boy.

The family was very cosy and offered everything they had. Their kitchen was like a store, with three big cupboards, two fridges, and beer to drink at any time. That was Germany: you didn't have to be rich to enjoy a good quality of life.

Merle explained that she had been divorced a few years before and now lived with her boyfriend. He was a baker, and I tried his bread, which was the tastiest I'd ever had—much better than the bread in France, I thought, even though French bread has such a fine reputation. The bread that night was baked with lemon and tasted better than a piece of cake.

The work was easy: vacuuming the living room, chopping wood, cutting some branches. The exchange was fair, as Merle never let me work more than four hours per day and gave me the weekends off.

Her ex often visited his family, always accompanied by his girlfriend and her kids. The kids all played with each other. I was very surprised by this kind of relationship after a divorce.

When I asked Merle about it, she said, 'It wasn't easy at the beginning, Martin. We worked hard to get things the way you see them now.'

I explained my current situation to Merle, and she found me some painting work to do for her neighbour for a few days. I earned enough to pay for a bus ticket to Copenhagen, the capital of Denmark. The couple I was to stay with in Denmark were called Leif and Marta. He was a psychotherapist, and she was a natural pharmacist. The work was all outdoors. It was the end of February and somewhat cold, but spring was coming.

It was a very long trip to Copenhagen. I walked to the train station, which was just a few hundred metres away. The first image I saw of this city reminded me of London in the 1960s, as I had seen a documentary about it before leaving my country. I had to buy some Danish kroner before buying the ticket. It wasn't necessary to go to the ticket window, as the machines offered the help I needed.

I took the train, and in an hour and a half, I arrived at Graested station, where Leif was waiting for me. He was driving a small car, and it was difficult to fit my suitcase on the back seat. He was a bit older than sixty, with white hair and a long beard, and he had small eyes that made him look more Chinese than Danish. After driving for ten minutes, we arrived in front of a large farmhouse—or at least what was left of a farm, some ruined buildings where horses and cows had lived many years ago. Leif's plan was to restore these buildings and turn them into a therapeutic centre where his clients could have complete therapy, including food and accommodation. Behind the farm was their house and lawn, with many tall trees and grass higher than one metre. His plan was also to have a small private lake made by digging a hole in the middle of the garden; there, his clients would be able to relax and meditate.

We walked around the property for twenty minutes, and then we entered the house. Inside I found a big mess. Shelves contained plenty of food, along with tools, all of them mixed together. In the corner near the fridge lay their dog. I didn't expect this, as I hadn't read about a dog in their profile.

'Come, Mischa!' said Leif. 'Martin, come and meet our little friend. We rescued her a few month ago. I know she was abused by her former owner. Some people don't even know how to take care of themselves, and then they try to have a pet. But now she's in the right hands.'

Leif picked up the dog and cuddled her neck, chuckling. 'Mischa, you good dog!'

Next, we entered the kitchen. My first impression was that I was in a French kitchen, and Leif agreed. He, too, was attracted to French history and culture. Beside the kitchen was a small dining room, and after a tight corridor we ended up in the living room, also of typical French nineteenth-century style. Leif built a fire in the chimney, even though the room was warm.

'Well, now I'll show you the room where you're gonna, Martin,' Leif said. 'It's just beside the door, over here.'

We walked towards the door, and my room was on the right side. I was a bit surprised to see how tiny a space I was to use for my stay, but Leif suggested that I could choose between that room and another one, in which was on the second floor.

Marta arrived just as I was putting my suitcase in the doorway to the room.

'Hello, Martin! Good to see you!'

'Happy to see you, Marta!'

'I did some quick shopping, Martin,' Marta said. 'I hope you like vegetables. How was your trip? Are you tired?'

'No, but I would like to arrange my stuff in the room, as Leif suggested.'

'OK. While I prepare dinner, you get settled,' she said. 'I'm sure you are exhausted after that long trip, sweetheart. What a stupid question to ask if you're tired! We're gonna have dinner in forty minutes. Afterwards, you can rest in your room for as long as you want.'

A big bowl of salad was served on the table. We had a short conversation. After dinner, I went to my room and lay down on the bed. I had a deep sleep till late morning. I woke up to some noises coming from the living room. It was already ten o'clock.

'Good morning, Martin!' said Leif while was cleaning the chimney. 'Did you sleep well?'

'Yes. I had a deep sleep. Sorry I woke up a bit late.'

'It's not late for us. We usually start the day at half past nine. Take it easy; it's your first day. You can go into the kitchen and help yourself to breakfast. You already saw where the fridge is. And don't forget the juice that Marta made for you!'

In the kitchen I saw a big glass of green juice. I tried it, but the taste wasn't what I expected. It wasn't a sweet fruit juice but a vegetable one. Some thin slices of bread were left on the bench. I took some butter and jam from the fridge, and some Danish cheese too, which I was curious to taste. I then joined Leif in the living room.

'Martin! That's a lot of bread on your plate,' Leif said with a chuckle.

'Well, I'm a bit hungry,' I answered, having no other justification, even though the slices were thin and small.

'After you are done, I'm gonna show you some of my future projects. There's one thing you can start today,' Leif said.

I thought I would just be doing some garden work while I was there, but the long list Leif showed me had a variety of jobs that I had never done before. They wanted me to stay for a minimum of three months, but I was excited to see Norway, so I didn't want to stay longer than a month.

It was an easy start in the garden: cutting grass, covering the plants with a large plastic sheet, and putting some heavy stones on the borders.

Afterwards, Marta came and suggested we do some more shopping. If I accompanied her, I could choose what I wanted. Most hosts offered what they had, but I now had the chance choose. The first item on my list was Nutella, even though I noticed it was double price it cost in other countries. I wasn't shy any more; working as a volunteer, I at least had to have my appetite satisfied.

My happiness didn't last too long, as Marta and Leif considered that 60 per cent of products in stores were replaced with chemicals. When we arrived home, Marta set all the stuff on the table. Leif cast a sideways glance at the biscuits and chocolates.

'He's a sugar boy! If he spends a few months with us, I'm sure he's gonna change his mind,' said Marta.

There were pictures of the family in the kitchen. I didn't like the way Marta's face looked in one of the pictures; she had a fake smile, and suddenly I had a bad feeling that something unpleasant was going to happen during my stay with them.

That evening, I helped Marta prepare dinner, cutting vegetables and setting the table in the living room, as they wanted to watch TV while we ate. It was one of Marta's favourite shows, called *The Fat Duck*, about one of the most famous restaurants in the world, situated in Bray, a small village in Great Britain.

I enjoyed dinner, with both of them sharing their knowledge and experiences. They spoke with such kindness that there was no room for any worry about something bad happening.

The next morning, I woke up a bit late. Leif was waiting for me outside. I grabbed some slices of bread, and I ran outside.

'Good morning, Leif! Sorry I'm late.'

'No, it's not late. You are right on time,' he said. 'Come, Martin. I'm gonna show you the work for today.'

A big pile of wood lay in the backyard. It came from a ruined house, so Leif got the wood for free.

'You see all this wood? Your job is to—'

'I have to cut all the wood into small pieces, right? Got it!' I interrupted, excited to start the work.

'Do you know how to use a chainsaw?' asked Leif.

'Erm, not too well; I only used one once.'

'OK, then, let me explain everything that you should and shouldn't do. We'll take it easy,' said Leif.

First, Leif taught me how to use the chainsaw in a safe way. He also suggested that an axe would be better and faster to use for the thinner pieces. After we cut the wood, we put the small pieces of wood into a wheelbarrow and brought it into a big room not far from the pile of wood. As the wood was still wet, needed to get it dry before putting it in the fireplace. This work became our routine every day, starting at half past nine and finishing at two o'clock. When Leif had clients, I worked alone.

Mischa accompanied me most of time, and it became harder to work, as she would bark when I didn't give her any attention. One day while working alone, I developed that strong headache again. Everything turned grey! I saw him standing with an axe, just like at the Hare Krishna community. Mischa just kept barking. I instantly put down the axe, and I ran inside the house.

Marta was in the kitchen. Without paying any attention to her, I grabbed a glass of water and drank it all at once.

'What happened, Martin?' asked Marta. 'Why that pale face? Did you see a ghost, maybe?'

Maybe I had done; maybe not. I didn't answer. Instead, I drank another glass of water.

'Where is Leif? I need to talk to him,' I said.

'He's busy at the moment with some clients,' Marta said. 'What's wrong, Martin? Are you OK, sweetheart? You can speak to me also, as I have much experience helping people. I'm sure I can help you too. So, please tell me. Is it something to do with Leif and me?'

'Oh no, Marta! Both of you have been very kind to me, and I'm very grateful. But it's not as simple as it looks. When I think about my travels and my future—for instance, wondering when I'm gonna be financially independent, able to buy a car—or wondering—'

'That's your ego talking to you!' she interrupted.

'Ego?!'

'You know, Martin, sometimes we are overwhelmed by routines anxieties, worries, and problems that cause us to disconnect from our higher self, which always has our best interests at heart. The voice of our higher self is often drowned out by the voice of the ego.'

'I wish I could turn back time. Only that can solve my problems,' I said.

'It's not reasonable to blame yourself for mistakes you have made in your past,' she continued. 'They were lessons you had to learn, and from these mistakes you begin teaching yourself compassion and forgiveness. We have to forgive ourselves because, after all, we tried to do the best we could at the time. The only moment you can change is the present, and I'm telling you that there are amazing resources within us. You have the courage, strength, compassion and love that you really need. You begin to understand your values and passions by learning about yourself, and then you can grow into the person you choose to be. Life will begin to flow easier.'

'Amazing resources, eh?'

'Yes, Martin. You are the only true judge of your self-worth; that's why you need to know how to validate yourself! No one else can understand your journey and your true purpose like you do! Believe me, you will never achieve your true purpose if you continually try to please others.'

'How do you know that I have strength and courage? Often I feel lost and afraid.'

She moved closer to me, whispering slowly, 'Don't be guided by fear, Martin. Be guided by love because the only guide which our higher self follows is love. You will never find true peace and happiness if you make judgements and decisions based on fear. You will follow the path of love only when you follow the voice of your higher self.'

'It's not easy when you find yourself in the middle of nowhere and have no control over your life.'

'Learning to go with the flow of life pushes us to be accepting instead of controlling. As human beings, we seek security in order to be able to control life; but, in truth, we will never control everything. Our idea is that things "must" be a certain way causes us to force ourselves to adapt to that way instead of accepting reality. To ensure that we are safe and secure, we often feel the need to control others, our relationships, and our problems. True love is never judgemental. Our relationships improve when we let everyone live their own lives in their own way. Then, we will not judge others, just do the best we can with our own lives. Our security comes when we accept life as it is because we then no longer need to control external factors.'

'Thank you, Marta. I'm sure this advice will help me. Now I have a better idea of how to fix myself.'

'You don't need fixing, sweetheart! That is not necessary, despite what you have learned from your family or your education; you are good enough as you truly are! Improving yourself doesn't enable your "spiritual growth". By following the path of your higher self, you shine your soul in the world, and that shows everyone your unique perceptions and gifts. But this only happens if you accept yourself as you are. You show yourself unconditional love and compassion. When you completely accept yourself, the negative and harmful thought patterns will begin to disappear, and you will be able shine with the nature of your true essential being.'

She kept talking and talking, and the time flew by. I just listened, having never heard any of these theories before.

I start to set the table, and Marta brought lunch.

Leif came in and rushed to the table, saying, 'Right on time! I'm bit hungry.'

'Are you done with the clients?' asked Marta.

'Of course I'm done; otherwise, I wouldn't be here! What kind of question is that?!'

'I meant, are you done for the day,' answered Marta.

'Yes, I'm completely done for the day. After lunch, I'll go and rest till late evening. I deserve it after all those hours of therapy and struggle.'

'Martin wanted to speak to you,' said Marta. 'He didn't seem quite well after work.'

'No, now I feel much better, Marta. Thank you, but no worries!' I answered, even though I thought that I should still speak to Leif.

'Well, if it's not something urgent, I would like to wait for tomorrow; as it will be Sunday, I'll have plenty of time.'

'Thank you, Leif! I appreciate it,' I said, a bit nervous when I thought about what I was going to tell him.

I lay down for a few hours. After I woke up, I went for a walk in the forest, meditating as I went. On the way back I noticed that I had gone too far. For a moment I felt lost. I started to rush, as it was dark and very quiet. Even in a safe place, I wouldn't like this kind of feeling. Afterwards, I saw the hazy light of the garners. I noticed the car wasn't in the yard. I entered the house through the front door and saw Mischa lying down. The kitchen was empty.

Suddenly Leif called down from the corridors upstairs, 'Hi, Martin. I started to worry about you. I thought maybe you were lost somewhere,' he said with a chuckle.

'Almost.'

'Marta will be late tonight because she's in a meeting,' continued Leif. 'Please open the fridge and help yourself. No one cooked dinner.'

I wasn't hungry. I just ate some biscuits and then went upstairs to lie down on my bed.

The next morning, I woke up late, as it was Sunday.

Marta was in the living room.

'Come have a seat, Martin,' she said. 'Leif will be here a bit later.'

We spend almost an hour watching TV shows, and then Marta started to yell for Leif.

Five minutes later, Leif appeared. I didn't expect that kind of attire. He was well dressed, just like when he met with his clients.

'Are you ready, Martin?' Leif asked. 'As I promised, we will talk today. Do you have something to tell me about yourself?'

'Yes, Leif. I'm ready.'

He had me sit in front of him, where the big table was on the left side of the living room, the usual place for his meetings with clients.

'All right now. Tell me whatever you wish, Martin—your problems, your worries, or whatever else you wish to share.'

I didn't know where to start.

'Well, I often have a headache,' I answered.

'That happen when we have stress, when we don't drink enough water, or—'

'I think it's something else,' I interrupted. 'Something I'm worried about.'

'So, what do you think it is? Please tell me everything.'

'Sometimes … when—' I hesitated, and my voice trailed off.

'Yes, what happens?' asked Leif, encouraging me to explain.

'You see me sitting here?'

'Yes, I see you.'

'But I'm not really here! I'm sitting over there and watching both of you and myself.'

From his eyes, I could tell that he felt a bit shocked to hear me say this.

'Well, I never heard of this before. I think that maybe you have the proof that the human body is just a machine,' said Leif.

'Do you believe in good and evil?' I asked.

'No, Martin! Such things are all in the mind! Now, let me explain to you the way I heal people with IFT therapy.'

He took a pencil and his notebook and started to write, continuing to talk and write at the same.

'All matter is composed of small particles. In between these particles there is a space, and on between this space is a vibration, which normally goes straight. When we are ill, have stress, or experience pain, this vibration becomes irregular, moving up or down instead of straight. To normalize this vibration, we have to create another vibration to stabilize the vibration inside the body. Now, Martin, put your hands in front of you, open your fingers, and clap your hands.'

He did this, and I repeated his movements.

'When we are in front of people, and we want to evitate, I suggest another hidden technique: cross your hands, and with two fingers tap the bottom of the smallest finger. This is supposed to be neither fast nor slow, but the same speed as the heartbeat. The Chinese devised this technique four thousand years ago. The second exercise consists of twisting your nipples in a clockwise motion. This helps to cleanse the body. Remember, always breathe with the stomach, so the organs below it can release anxiety. This breathing technique will accompany each exercise. The third exercise consists of tapping your upper chest with two fingers. Take a deep, deep breath till you can't hold it any more, and then start to release the air halfway; wait for three seconds and then totally release the air.'

'How many times do I have to repeat the exercises?' I asked.

'I often get this question from my clients,' Leif said. 'Do the exercises as often as you can. After you do them, your body will feel tired, and that will mean it is repairing itself.'

I was so excited, thinking that, perhaps, I had found the solution to my problems. I went into my room and began to do the exercises. Breathing with the stomach immediately made me feel tired, but Leif had mentioned that this was a good sign, so I continued doing the exercises.

Sunday ended too fast for a day off.

The next morning, I felt too lazy to start with something hard.

Marta understood, and when I went outside, she called, 'Eh, Martin! What do you thing about doing some shopping with me? Maybe it will be an easier way for you to start your day.'

'Sounds great,' I said.

I was a bit surprised by the way Marta could understand how I was feeling, even offering a solution for what might help me to feel better.

Leif heard our conversation and ran outside, saying, 'Where are you going, Marta? I need Martin to help me in the garden. I have—'

'We'll be back in less than an hour,' she interrupted.

'Don't spend too much, because I have bills to pay!'

'I'm going to get Mischa's food; that's all!' screamed Marta through the car window.

Leif closed the gate when we left the yard.

'We have money, Martin, but Leif, as always, is complaining. Now that we have a big project to begin, he's having too much stress.'

When I didn't respond, Marta asked, 'Did you ever heard of Anita Moorjani?'

'No.'

'She was the best-selling author of the book *Dying to Be Me*. After suffering with cancer for three years and eight months, her organs began to shut down. Then, she slipped into a deep coma for thirty-one hours. She passed into the afterlife after being sent to hospital. I heard a bit about the experiences explained to Leif, that's why I'm telling you this.'

'So, do you believe it?'

'Of course I believe it. All we do in this life is nothing!'

Boom! The highest point of view of life. What we do in this life is nothing! What are we supposed to think about criminals, then? I didn't share my opinion; I just let Marta continue talking.

As always, she kept on repeating, 'We know everything.'

We stopped close to an old wooden bar that looked more like a garner. We sat in the corner, at a small round table. I ordered hot chocolate, as Marta said they were pros at it.

I didn't see any sugar on my plate. Without thinking, I said, 'So stupid!'

'Don't judge people, Martin,' Marta said. 'The words we express mirror our inner selves!'

I laughed and asked her, 'What do you think about someone going around and saying, "I want to kill people"?'

'Maybe he wanted to kill himself.'

'Well that's not what happened.'

'Take my sugar, Martin. The chocolate is sweet enough for me.'

The pet store was just a five-minute drive away. Marta bought a big box of meat, coming from Germany. She had ordered the dog food a week before. I helped her put the box in the car.

On the way back, we drove near a river. I noticed some ruined buildings.

Observing me, Marta said, 'Do you see all these ruins, Martin? A long time ago, witches lived around here and practised sorcery. When the witch-hunting started, a lot of them were executed and burned alive. It's such a shame; they were just some smart women trying to invent and develop medicine.'

When we got back to the house, I suggested that I could prepare Mischa's food. I put some vegetables in the mixer and then added some fresh meat. This was the first time I ever saw a dog eat vegetables.

Leif called for me to come outside to help him in the garden. I had to put some heavy stones around a plastic cover that he used to protect some plants, as it was still cold and windy.

After an hour's work, I was free to go to my room and check my emails. I got a positive answer from a cheese factory I had written to while I was in Germany. The factory was in southern Norway, not far from the capital, Oslo.

I surfed the Internet for an hour, visiting different websites, but I did not give any confirmation, as I wasn't yet sure which day I was going to leave. I only had easy work left on Leif and Marta's list, so why not speak with them first and then decide when to leave? Their attitude till now had made me feel safe, so I wasn't worried about telling them I planned to leave soon, even though probably weren't expecting such short notice.

I left my room and went through the living room, where I saw Marta in front of her laptop.

As I got closer her, she suddenly turned, saying, 'Ah, Martin! Here you are!'

I immediately noticed her agitation as she instantly closed her laptop and flashed a smile which I didn't like. It seemed fake, like the smile in the photo in the kitchen; besides, it wasn't necessary at that moment.

'I was having a quick look at some recipes I want to use tomorrow for lunch. Are you curious to see them?' asked Marta.

'Yes, maybe. Where is Leif?' I said, a bit nervous. 'I want to speak to him about the work I'm finishing.'

'Finishing?! I thought you just started! Are you going to leave, maybe? Did you know that your minimum stay is three months?' said Marta with the same fake smile.

'Well, yes. That is what I want to talk about with Leif,' I said.

'Leif is upstairs in his room. He's gonna need you to get a table from the storage room,' she said.

I went upstairs and saw the door was half open.

'Come in, Martin!' said Leif. 'As you can see, it's a big mess in here. Instead of arranging everything in here, I'm gonna use another room for storage, kind of like a huge bureau. We have plenty of space, so I'm gonna choose a room with a view of the garden. First, I want to have a table and chairs. I have two chairs here, but I need a table. Can you give me a hand to bring it from our storage room to here?'

'Yes, sure,' I said.

'First, we have to dismantle the table, as it is too big to be fit through the doors.'

I followed him to the storage room, and suddenly he lifted his right arm in greeting. There was a plane flying many miles away, so high in the sky that it was difficult to even hear it. I didn't expect his strange reaction.

He explained himself, saying, 'I'm used to saying hello every time they pass overhead. I'm weird!'

'Sometimes I can be weird too,' I said to console him.

'Welcome to the family!' said Leif.

When we got to the storage room, I had to clean the table and then dismantle it, while Leif looked at the job I'd done with the chopped wood.

Seeing the huge pile, he said, 'I'm surprised by your effort, Martin. I knew you were hard worker, but this is more than expected. We'll take it easy for the next few days—maybe just some painting work.'

After settling the table in his new office, we moved the chairs around it.

Leif then suggested another interesting technique of IFT therapy: tapping the forehead with two fingers, then the temples, and the lips, upper and lower; then, using the right side of the biggest and smallest fingers of the left hand to tap the bottom of the chest. During this process, was advised to repeat a phrase concerning the problem at hand. As Leif explained, the solution of IFT therapy consisted of going through the issue. For example, people with cancer and afraid of dying had to repeat, 'I have cancer; I have cancer. I'm gonna die; I'm gonna die.' The second part of this method consisted of using the same tapping technique but adjusting the phrase: for example, 'I have cancer, but I love and accept myself.'

'How many times should I try this?' I asked.

'I guess you know already my advice about the exercises. When you increase your effort, the problem will gradually resolve itself. I do not guarantee success in 100 per cent of cases, of course. If you want to improve yourself in the right way, Martin, you have to follow your heart. The true brain of our body is not the brain at all; it's the heart. The brain does what the heart says. At the end of the day, there's nothing right and nothing wrong in this world! Everything is as it should be.'

After finishing the conversation with Leif, I went downstairs and saw Marta in the kitchen, preparing dinner. I asked her if she needed help.

'You can go and relax in your room,' she said. 'I'm gonna ask Leif to help me. I'll call when dinner is ready.'

I didn't expect her cold tone of voice. I went to my room and opened my emails again. I replied to the cheese factory, explaining in one brief sentence that I would arrive in a few days to stay with them. I wanted to be sure I had a set destination to go to if something went wrong with Leif and Marta. After Marta's behaviour earlier, I wouldn't be surprised if things became unpleasant.

I now wished to go forward with my journey to Norway, choosing the most interesting places and towns there. As I surfed websites, the first on the list appeared to be the city of Bergen, which I was fascinated and curious about; I definitely wanted to see it.

After an hour of surfing and waiting for Marta to call me, I went to see if dinner was ready. Marta and Leif were sitting in the living room, relaxing and watching TV. They'd already eaten dinner.

'Hey, Martin! Come join us. We were waiting for you. Here's some leftover rice and veggies,' said Marta in an evil, sarcastic way. Sarcastic because there was nothing left on the table, and evil because of the way she looked at me.

I sat in my usual spot and started to watch TV, waiting to see if they would say something about my departure. Leif looked very cold and serious.

After twenty minutes of silence, Marta switched off the TV and said, 'Now we can talk, Martin. Please tell us the truth! I know you have some plans you didn't tell us about.'

'How do you know about my plans?!' I asked, surprised.

'We know everything!' she said. 'So, if you want to leave, do it!'

'Well, first, I need some help—'

'Help?!' she interrupted. 'We've already helped you! What do you mean?'

'I need to find some paying jobs,' I said. 'I need to earn some money to pay for my trip to Norway.'

'Well, I don't think we can help you with that,' she replied. 'But, of course, we could send you somewhere close to here, as a volunteer.'

'Yes, we could bring you there and tell the people who you are!' added Leif in a brusque tone.

'We can't help you with money, Martin,' said Marta matter-of-factly. 'We don't have any left. We have no money! No, no, no!'

I couldn't say a word at that moment. I was quite shocked. Although I had sensed a change in Marta's demeanour, I still didn't expect such coldness from her and Leif. I felt very disappointed, as I'd been confident in our relationship till earlier that day.

How could this be? I wondered.

I went to my room, slowly closed the door, and lay down on the bed. All I wanted was to leave soon as possible, but it was too late now would be very difficult to hitch-hike. I had to wait till the morning, without having even a minute of sleep. At six o'clock, I started to pack everything, and in half an hour I was ready to go, but I didn't want to leave without saying goodbye to them. At eight o'clock, I heard noises in the living room. I went there and saw Marta, dressed and ready.

'Is everything packed, Martin?' she asked.

'Yes,' I said. 'How did you know about my plans?'

'I hacked your computer! Yes, I did! Are you a gamer? Is your username Jokerino?'

'You hacked my computer?!' I exclaimed.

I was shocked. This was too much.

'Now I'm gonna accompany you to a village not far from here. We know some people who need volunteers!'

'What's all this noise?!' screamed Leif from the door. 'Are you still here?!'

'I'm gonna send him—'

'No, Marta!' I interjected. 'You are not sending me anywhere! I'm leaving and not ever coming back to this place!'

I grabbed my suitcase and ran outside. Escaping from the Witch and Gandalf! Finally, I was back to my plan of going to Norway! Afraid? No, I wasn't at all. I had never felt such freedom in my entire life as I did in that moment—away from them, on the street, and ready for my next adventure.

I walked and walked, lifting my thumb once on a while. Cars were very rare in this part Denmark, or maybe it was just early. After I walked for an hour, finally, someone stopped behind me. It was an old lady in a red car. I introduced myself, and she offered me a ride till Copenhagen. She was going to visit her niece in the centrum, where I could stop and continue on to Sweden. I told her briefly about my trip to Norway, and she suggested some interesting places for me to see in Copenhagen. The first she suggested was Nyhavn, the central harbour; the site of the Little Mermaid; Christiania, etc. I wasn't sure if time would permit me to see all of these in one day, but I definitely wanted to stop in the centrum. She parked near the tourism office and suggested that I get a map. Such a kind lady! We said goodbye and wished either well.

I took a complimentary map and went straight to the harbour, an area consisting of two blocks of restored historic buildings built around the canal. There were many restaurants all around, and two canal boat tours departed from this place. The restaurants seemed to be expensive. I saw also some shops and hotels filled with tourists. After spending forty minutes there, I changed direction, walking to the other side of the town.

I was also curious to see Christiania, which I'd heard about ever since my time in Belgium. Simon told me about this place, as he had been there before coming to Belgium. At the entrance, I noticed a beautiful fairy-tale painting, where a lot of people were taking pictures. Inside was a mix of homemade houses, bare and rustic workshops, art galleries, music venues, cheap and organic eateries—all surrounded by beautiful nature. As I read at the entrance, it was a society within a society, created in 1973, in an army hall bringing aggressive and provocative dance music. After twenty minutes of walking, I started to dislike this environment. I immediately noticed drug dealers and heavy drug users, the worst part of this place. There was too much noise, and it was smoky and smelly. I turned to walk back to the entrance, and a young lady pushed me. I didn't say anything; I just continued walking. She wore a ripped T-shirt and looked half dead.

When I reached the entrance again, I noticed two young Italians taking selfies in front of the painting.

Suddenly one of them said, '*Ey, Marko, fai presto che dobbiamo correre in Swedia!*' ('Hey, Marko, we have to hurry to Sweden.')

I decided to go and talk to them in Italian. Maybe they could offer me a lift to Sweden. I greeted them, smiling, and briefly introduced myself, telling them why I planned to go to Norway.

They agreed to let me travel with them, as they were excited to see Oslo also, along with some other interesting places in Scandinavia.

Marko asked me if I had a passport and the rest of the necessary documents.

I said yes. I lied, but I didn't want to miss this chance; maybe I knew better than they about the Schengen area. As they were just beginning to see Christiania, they suggested that I wait near the car, which was parked not far from there. I waited not more than forty minutes.

They came back and set my suitcase in the trunk. They were rushing to Sweden, and I was happy to join them, speaking Italian all the way to northern Scandinavia.

We travelled across the Øresund Bridge, the longest combined road-and-rail bridge in Europe. After eight kilometres, we reached Malmö, the first town in Sweden. As expected, our passports were inspected, and I still hoped to reach Norway feeling the same way I did up to that point.

I was telling my story to the Italians, and they became very curious to know about the way I was travelling and meeting all these people across the countries I visited. After three hours of driving, we decided to stop at Gottenburg City. I was expecting a longer stay, like going in the centrum, sitting in a bar or restaurant, taking selfies, and so on. But that did not happen. The Italian guys were in a hurry, and all we did was just some shopping in the big stores outside the town.

'Oh, look! Is that an Albanian flag?' asked Marko.

I turned my head towards the other side of the road, and I saw an Albanian flag on top of the store. We decided to go and shop for some traditional Albanian food, which I missed a lot. I greeted the workers, and it felt a bit strange to pronounce Albanian words after all this time. All we got was just some smoked meat. We quickly turned to the car and went all the way to Oslo without making any other stops.

Marko took pictures from the window.

I was feeling a bit tired and for a moment I closed my eyes.

'Tok, tok! Wake up, Martin! Welcome to Oslo. I mean, to Norway!'

The Italian guys were already outside. They opened the trunk and pulled out my suitcase.

I couldn't believe that I was in front of Oslo train station. I said goodbye to the Italians, and I took the tram to Gardermoen Airport. The village I was going to was forty minutes from there. It didn't take me to long to arrive at the airport, and I was hoping to find free Wi-Fi. All I had to do was send an email to Therese, the owner of the factory. They weren't expecting my arrival today, as I hadn't yet given them any date. I had their address, and by using a maps app, I could find the bus to their nearest stop.

After leaving the airport, I observed nature all around me, a beautiful landscape with long, green fields. It was a sunny day, and for a moment it reminded me France, even though I was in the coldest country of Europe. I went outside the bus, and I asked someone for Therese's farm. He didn't answer, but when I mentioned the cheese factory, he pointed to an old white house up the hill. I had to pull my suitcase for more than three hundred metres to reach the farm. I noticed an old couple in the field, planting vegetables. I approached them slowly.

'Is this Therese's farm?' I asked them.

'Yes, it is, and Therese is my name.'

'I'm Martin. I sent an invitation a few day ago and—'

'Ah, Martin! Yes, I know you. I remember your face from your profile. I saw on work exchange, but I didn't expect you today!'

'Sorry, Therese, but—'

'No, don't be sorry. You have come right on time, my dear, as we need lot of help to maintain this farm. Come, let me introduce my husband, Robert.'

He looked a bit older than Therese. He wore round glasses and held an old hat in his hand.

'Martin, let me finish first, and then I'll join you inside the house,' Therese said. 'The other helpers should be there, asking or doing something else; I don't know.'

'Thank you, Therese. I'm happy to join your farm!'

I went close to the house, and at the entrance, I heard two guys shouting and laughing. They saw me and greeted me. I set my suitcase at the main door. The first one to shake my hand was Tom from Germany, and then Ariel from Ukraine. Suddenly a young lady appeared. She was called Jess, a pretty blonde with short hair from the Netherlands. We sat down in the living room, which was smaller than I expected, but when Tom opened the back doors, I saw a big kitchen fully equipped with appliances and a lot of gadgets hanging on the walls. We started to chat and talk about the farm and the cheese factory.

When I mentioned that I was going to stay longer than two weeks, Jess interrupted, saying, 'Two weeks?! Maybe that's too long to stay here, Martin.'

I was surprised by the way she said that.

The house was big and comfortable, and I had a good feeling about Therese and Robert. We set the table, and after a few minutes Robert joined us. He suggested to start dinner, as Therese was busy on the phone. She arrived twenty minutes later, apologizing for her lateness and explaining that her niece had called and she hadn't spoken with her in a year.

I was enjoying the warm soup which had Jess made, accompanied by a salad, some garlic toasted bread, and some desserts to finish.

Therese started to ask about my trip and my experience with Marta and Leif, but she wasn't interested in hearing my long story. She looked very tired and soon left the table, accompanied by Robert.

I suddenly felt a cold atmosphere. I didn't hear anything about house rules, weekly programmes, or even simple discussions about their routine.

The sleeping room was on the second floor, with four beds. One remained empty, and Jess slept in another room.

Tom set the alarm for half past eight the next morning. We said goodnight. For me, that was the perfect time to start the day.

In the morning I washed my face and brushed my teeth. It was only eight o'clock. I went down to the living room, and I saw Jess arranging some tools. I noticed that no one had done the dishes last night.

Therese came into the living room at a quarter past eight and asked for a copy of my passport.

I hesitated, as no one had asked for that before.

'Do you accept my driving licence as ID?' I asked.

'Yes, no problem. You know, I set some rules to keep my place safe and secure; I mean, I have nothing personal against you,' Therese explained.

'Everyone does it; I did it,' said Jess.

I gave my driving licence to Therese.

Five minutes later, she came back and started to explain the work programme. It was all written out on a big piece of cardboard.

I approached, and I noticed a twisted face in the corner. I asked Therese what it was.

'That's *The Scream*, the famous painting of Edvard Munch. He was Norwegian,' Therese explained and then said, 'Martin, in the cheese factory we start work at nine o'clock in the morning. Jess will help with packing the cheese, and you will do something else. I'm gonna explain as soon as we get there.'

'What's about Tom and Ariel?' I asked, curious to know about their jobs.

'We're gonna help Robert in the garage,' answered Tom from where he stood on the stairs.

We quickly finished breakfast, and at exactly 8.55 a.m., I went to the factory. At the main door we dressed in white uniforms, took off our shoes, and put on some clean boots. Before going in, I was told to wash my hands with alcohol soap. The first room, which was the smallest, was called the packing room; this was where Jess was going to work. In the second room, which was a bit bigger, I saw two wooden pools filled with dirty water; this was where the cheese had to soak for a few days. The third room was ten times bigger than the second; this was where the cheese produced in the factory was stored on the shelves lining the walls.

All I had to do was turn the cheese and wash it with vinegar. It was an easy job, but seeing all those shelves, I guessed it could take me at least four to five hours to finish. After terminating each raw cheese, I also had to change the water. I was almost done when Jess came and interrupted me. It was one o'clock in the afternoon, lunchtime.

I saw Robert sitting outside in the veranda. Tom and Ariel were bringing some boxes with food. Some salad and cheese were served, along with a bottle of orange juice.

'Martin, I forgot to mention that here we serve vegetarian,' said Therese.

I was surprised, but it didn't bother me, even though I was not a vegetarian.

I didn't touch the salad but I tried some sort of cheese. The first I took was the brown cheese; I became more curious to try it, as I had never seen this kind of cheese before. From the first bite it became my favourite, and I couldn't stop eating it. As the rest of the table was a bit poor, the cheese was worth it.

It was a beautiful view surrounded by mountains behind, a small lake on the left, and fields all around—a landscape rich in nature.

'Do you own all this land, Robert?' I asked.

'Yes, we do! Half of the lake is also ours, and the road on the right divides my land from my neighbour's; he's teaching me to hunt, by the way. We have plenty of mass around here, fresh meat from mother Norway.'

'Are you Norwegian, Robert?'

'No, I'm not. I grew up in Amsterdam, in the Netherlands, and there I met Therese. She's Norwegian, but at that time she was working as a waitress in one of my boats. I had two sailing boats for tourists. I sold the boats, and with the money I bought this small piece of paradise.'

'Small! Ha!' I said, laughing.

'You know, the land is quite cheap here. Five million people live in Norway, and it has the same amount of land as Germany. When I met the previous owner of this land, he was worried about the cheese business. At that time, he was producing just three tons of cheese per year, but now we produce four times more than that—around twelve tons of cheese—including Italian and traditional Norwegian.'

I started helping Tom to put back what was left from the table. It was a big fridge, but inside I saw just some vegetables and potatoes, all half spoilt.

After a five-minute break, I went back to the factory to finish my work. It took me a bit more than one hour. I took off the uniform and boots, dressed in my own clothes and shoes, and went outside.

'Hey, Martin!' Robert called from the garage.

I was hoping for no more work, as I was feeling tired.

'Can you help Tom to lift the old tires on the shelves?'

'Yes.'

'And after you are done with that, you both can join Ariel to finish with the door which needs some repairs, and that's all I ask for today!'

After Robert left, I asked Tom about working time.

'We usually work six hours per day and have weekends off.'

'Is it hard work?'

'No, but sometimes I spend more than six hours, maybe six and half or seven. Till now we have done mostly painting, profiting from the nice weather.'

We finished with the tires and joined Ariel on the right side of the garage. It was the biggest garage I had ever seen—almost twice as big as the house. Ariel was fixing the door set on the table.

'Right on time guys!' Ariel said.

'Why?' asked Tom.

'Ha ha ha!' We both laughed

'It's not funny. Come on, let's put this door back in place!'

'Aa-u-gh! Now I got it,' answered Tom.

It was quite heavy, but I wasn't surprised, given the size of the door.

During the afternoon I took a nap. Tom did the same. When I woke up, I noticed I'd slept more than an hour. Tom was still sleeping.

I went down to the living room, where I met Jess. She offered me a tea, and I was excited to share my story with her. I was surprised when I discovered the reason why Jess had come here: permaculture, not the factory.

'Yes, I was studying, and I also became curious to see moss and explore the wildlife.'

'I didn't know they also practise that here,' I said.

'Permaculture is like taking care of the plants, but in a natural way; you have to first know the earth, which decides or chooses the kind of plant that she wants to grow, and—'

'Yes, I know about permaculture,' I interrupted, excited to share what I'd learned in Belgium. 'Do you know about hugobeds?'

'I know a bit, but I've never done it,' Jess said.

I talked to Jess for more than forty minutes, and she was staring at me. I liked her face, and now I was aware that sharing my story was a good way to attract girls.

'Hi, guys! How you doing?' Ariel said as he came in.

'We're talking,' Jess said.

I guessed Ariel had been upstairs, sleeping.

'OK,' Ariel said.

He took a bottle of water from the fridge and sat close to her.

'So far, what were you talking about? I'm curious also to know about you, Martin' Ariel said and put his hand on Jess's neck.

I wasn't sure, but when Jess touched Ariel's hand, it became obvious that they were in relationship. It was like a slap on my face.

I went outside. The sky was grey. It was a good chance for rain, but I wanted to do some walking, as that had become my habit, and I needed to stay a bit alone. I went close to the lake. It was so quiet. It didn't least even two minutes, and the rain started. I went back to the house, and I saw Robert outside. I asked him if I could fish in my free time.

'You can fish in two ways: with a net or a fishing rope. You can find both in the garage,' Robert said.

Tom and Ariel sat in the living room. It was quiet, and I didn't say a word either.

Suddenly Jess came in. She was all wet, wearing a thin, transparent white shirt and tight pants. After Milena, she was the sexiest girl I had met in this exchange. All three of us stared at her.

'Where were you?' asked Ariel.

'Down in the river, swimming.'

'Swimming?!'

She went upstairs, and I was still staring at her back—that transparent shirt and tight pants.

Ariel was staring at me.

'Martin, want to see my blog tonight?' Tom asked. 'I mean, I have been to Norway twelve times, and I have taken some pictures and videos of the coolest places I visited. After dinner, we'll be in the living room. You can join if you want.'

'Yes, sure. I would like to!' I said.

Robert and Therese didn't come for dinner. They were living in a house apart, and it became usual to not see them around.

Tom connected his device to TV. His blog began with some pictures he'd taken six years ago, when he arrived in Norway for the first time, accompanied with some small descriptions. I had heard and seen some images on the Internet, but watching the details of his blog made me believe that I was in the wildest and most attractive country I could possibly be. That beautiful view of Pulpit Rock, high mountains and fjords, the highest waterfall of Vettisfossen, the iconic Rock of Trolltunga, ending with the magical islands of Lofoten. Jess and I remained fascinated. I had a great desire to visit all these places, but first I had to make a plan for my future hosts all the way up to northern Norway.

The next day, I didn't go to the factory. I had to join Tom and Ariel to build a fence. Robert came with his crane, holding some grand posts. This was another way of building a fence, but following the same plan I had made before with smaller pieces. It was hard work carrying all those heavy posts more than two metres long. The purpose of the fence was to protect Robert's land from wild animals. I didn't know he also owned five horses and twenty-five sheep. Now I understood better what Therese had told me when I arrived: they really needed help to maintain this big farm. It started to rain, and we were still working. During lunch, Robert suggested that we do different type of jobs, as the work with the fence was a bit hard. On sunny days, we were told to paint and help Therese in the factory. In the afternoon it was still raining, but that didn't mean we were done. The new job consisted of cleaning the building next to Therese's house. I thought it was another garner, but after passing the entrance with a shining refurbished oak floor, I saw a big room fully equipped with modern conveniences: a pool table, some red leather furniture, and a tennis table in the corner. In the smaller room next to it were some fitness equipment and a modern sauna. The garner was transformed magically in a fairy-tale room. We spent three hours cleaning, but most of the time playing.

Therese was standing at the entrance and observing. I didn't hear her come in because the volume of the stereo was high. Tom switched it off.

'I thought you were cleaning,' Therese said, but she was smiling. 'I'm not angry, because I wanted you to spend some of your free time. Tomorrow is the weekend!'

'Yes, we know!' answered Jess.

Therese, still smiling, said, 'Enjoy!'

I didn't expect that answer from Jess, and I became curious to know the reason for it.

'Yes, I came here once. I was with a couple from New Zealand who left after two days,' Jess said. 'Why two days?'

'Therese kicked them out, as she wasn't satisfied with their job. She's a bit weird!' said Ariel. 'She once told me that they had to close her Facebook account because they thought she had a connection with the CIA.'

'She's crazy!' said Jess as she left the room.

I left too.

Tom and Ariel stayed a bit longer to finish their tennis game.

During the weekend, we spent most of our time inside the house. I started to make a plan to choose a host close to Pulpit Rock. At the beginning of April, I had to move away, as it was perfect weather in Norway to visit certain places. I exchanged emails with a host called Josh. The job consisted of taking care of his dog (a walk of one hour per day) and watching his house while he was traveling in southern Europe for a few weeks. It was the easiest exchange I could find. As he was leaving on 27 April, I had to search for someone else till that date. I was curious to see bigger towns, as the job on the farms had become less interesting. In Kristiansand, a town in south-eastern Norway, a mother was asking for help taking care of her two boys, four and five years old. It reminded the experience with Leon, in the monastery, but would that be as simple as it seemed? I sent an email describing myself in a few words, as I wasn't sure if she could accept me for the dates I wanted. She accepted me, and it seemed that she was very happy to have me as a volunteer. Now that I had a complete profile and a lot of positive comments left from previous hosts, it made it easier for me to be accepted.

On Monday we started with painting, as it was a good weather. I asked Therese if she could find me some paying job as a solution for my next trip, to Kristiansand. She agreed, but by her face, I could tell she wasn't happy to hear this.

Next day, I had to work with a chainsaw, cutting branches. Robert stayed close by, watching.

'Not like that! You told me you knew how to use it!' he shouted.

'Yes, I know! I have used it before coming here!' I answered, sure that I was doing a proper job.

The week became more boring when Jess and Ariel left for Ukraine. Tom was happy to stay on, though, even alone.

It was rainy when Therese came and asked me to do some painting.

'Painting?!' I said.

'You gonna paint the cheese inside the factory,' she said.

It was easier than painting walls.

Next day, I had to cut the grass.

Therese came and observed. 'Martin! Look at what you left behind! The grass is not straight, and some parts you didn't cut at all! Please, if you don't know how to do a job this simple, I can't use you for anything!'

It wasn't my fault. I knew how to cut grass, but it was still wet.

I understood that I couldn't get money from them, and I didn't say anything.

The trip to Kristiansand was too long to hitch-hike, and I was too tired to try at the moment. I had to find paying jobs from the neighbours. First, I asked Robert for permission, and he agreed.

That weekend, I went down the road to the nearest neighbour. The job consisted of cutting branches and cleaning the garden. I finished in four hours, as I knew how to the work. They were very satisfied and paid me six hundred krones (sixty-two euros). I was happy, as I didn't expect that much money for such a brief time working.

When I told Tom, his answer surprised me: the minimum pay was 150 krones per hour.

'You should be satisfied because for that kind of job you received the right amount!' said Tom.

Of course I was satisfied, but I found out that a bus ticket to my destination was a bit less than the pay I had received.

On Sunday it was difficult for me to wake up. I slowly opened my eyes and asked myself, 'Where am I?! Am I in France or Denmark? Where am I? Where?!'

It was a very strange feeling, and I closed my eyes and fell back to sleep.

I was going to leave in two days. At half past seven on Tuesday morning, I packed my stuff. Tom waited for me in the living room. He had woken up early to accompany me to the train station, and I appreciated it. I wanted to prepare some food for my long trip, so I was in the kitchen. When I opened the fridge, I saw it was full. From what I remembered, last night it was almost empty.

'Didn't get it yet, Martin?!' Tom called from the living room. 'She gets all the food from the garbage.'

'You knew this?!' I asked.

'Of course. We all knew it. In Norway they throw out even good-quality food. This is how I lived in Lofoten for two weeks, sleeping in my car and getting food for free. It doesn't bother me, you know; at least I don't have to pay for my stay.'

I went back to Oslo in the same way I had arrived at the farm, and then I took the train from Oslo to Kristiansand. It was the most comfortable train I had ever been on, even though I was seated in the second-class section. It was a beautiful trip, taking hours.

At two o'clock that afternoon, I was waiting at the bus station. Camilla, the mother of the kids, had suggested I wait till half past two, as her husband was coming to pick me up. He was called Arrid, and he picked me up even earlier. I introduced myself, and I set my luggage in the back of the car. He was driving a Nissan Leaf, an electric car that was also the most common car in Norway. It looked more like a giant frog than a car, but, as Arrid explained, comparing the price and comfort, it was surely the most economical car to buy, as drivers paid less in tax and nothing at all to go through the tunnels.

We drove through the city centre. It was an interesting town, much different than Oslo. No skyscrapers or high buildings, but traditional wooden houses and historical monuments. I was also impressed to see a lot of American cars, compared to the other countries I had been to.

We got to the house, which seemed to be the most modern I could imagine: half wood and half glass, with an amazing view of the sea. When Arrid opened the garage, I was astonished. Inside was a beautiful 1960s Cadillac. It seemed like a new message: 'Welcome to North America'.

After going into the house through the main door, we entered the living room. All modern! Arrid switched on the fire with a remote control. In front of the sofa was a seventy-inch TV. On the right was the kitchen, also modern.

Two minutes later, Arrid called the kids to come down from upstairs. Two beautiful boys rushed downstairs to shake my hand and introduced themselves. They spoke Norwegian, and I didn't know a word of the language yet. I told this to Arrid, he said that wouldn't be necessary because my stay consisted mostly of just being present in the house when he and Camilla weren't home, plus driving the boys to kindergarten. (As it turned out, the first two days I hardly had anything to do, as Arrid was home the entire time.)

When Camilla arrived, she started to explain some more details about my stay, which was to include cleaning the house and putting the kids to bed before seven o'clock in the evening. (The last one proved more difficult, as they always wanted to stay awake longer so they could play.) Each morning, I also had to get them dressed and drive them to kindergarten. This was easy, as it was only a fifteen-minute drive. It was a routine which I became used to very quickly.

I noticed that Arrid slept on the sofa in the living room and Camilla slept upstairs. Often I would hear them shouting and fighting, but I couldn't understand anything they said in Norwegian. The kids were very happy with my company, and I liked them, but all the hours I worked every day and night seemed like hard work to me. I had a good relationship with Arrid, but not with Camilla. Sometimes she came home late, and sometimes she did not come home at all. Once, she was gone for two whole days.

One evening when I was talking to her, she said, 'Oh, Martin! It's not easy, you know. I didn't want to have kids, but it happened!'

I couldn't agree with what she said, and I remained a bit disappointed by her attitude.

One night, I sat in the living room drinking beers with Arrid. Camilla was still out, and the kids were sleeping. He seemed unhappy, as the relationship between him and Camilla was over. They were getting divorced and dividing in half all their expenses—but not the house. Arrid said that the house would belong to Camilla and her boyfriend. Camilla was inheriting a fish-farming company from her father, and her high salary would allow her to easily afford to live her life exactly the way she wanted to. Arrid was very quiet after saying that, and I felt sorry for him and the kids.

Once, Camilla came into the house, accompanied by her boyfriend. She introduced him to the kids for the first time. The oldest understood more about the situation and took a picture of his family, crying whilst holding the camera.

I was vacuuming the house when Arrid came to me and asked, 'How long do you want to stay with us, Martin?'

'Till 27 April,' I answered, knowing that Camilla and I had already agreed upon this before my arrival.

'You could stay longer if you wish. Do you want to? The kids love you.'

'Yes, I know,' I said.

'So, tell me, where are you planning to go afterwards?' he asked.

'I'm going to Stavanger and moving northwards later on. Bergen, maybe.'

'Bergen! It's still one of my favourite cities after travelling through all of Europe. I wish you good luck!' he said.

'Thanks, Arrid.'

'Ah! I have a friend in Bergen, Martin. He teaches martial arts. His name's Dag. Maybe he needs some help. I'm not sure, as I haven't talked to him since last year, but I'll give you his address and email. He also has a website. I suggest you have a look if you are interested in learning some martial arts. Tell him that I gave you his contact information.'

'Thank you, Arrid, I will!'

I was happy about this news. I went to my room, opened my laptop, and visited Dag's website. I saw a big guy with a ruddy face, posing like a Viking, holding a stick. I always searched for people to teach me; I wanted to learn. When the Vikings went to fight with ninjas, guess who won? The Vikings! I couldn't imagine having a Viking teach me martial arts. I sensed Bergen would become my favourite city and learning martial arts would be a dream come true.

My last day with Arrid and the kids arrived too quickly, and was time to say goodbye. I had enjoyed staying with them and now I was ready for my next adventure: Stavanger, the oil capital of Norway.

My new host, Josh, was waiting for me at the bus station. He was American, and his wife was from Germany. They had been in Norway for ten years, earning a good living to maintain their family, with two kids, seventeen and eighteen years old. Josh worked as a guide in a tourism office in the city centre and promised me some paid work doing translations from English to French. I was going to be paid half the professional rate, but it was still a great deal of money. I soon found out that I could earn more than ten thousand krones (eleven hundred euros).

The first day of my arrival I told Josh that the reason I had come to Stavanger was to see Pulpit

Rock. The second day, he took me there, as they had to leave for Spain the following day. We took the ferry from Stavanger to Tau, and from there we drove to the rock. It was a ripper hike of two hours which gave me the greatest and most awe-inspiring view.

'Simply impressive!' I said with a sigh.

Of course, it became one of my best experiences.

The days passed quickly, and all I had to do was walk the dog, near the forest. The rest of the day I spent writing translations.

I didn't get any answer from Dag, and so I had to write to someone else close to Trolltunga, following my plan to head northwards. After waiting two days, I didn't get any answer from them either. Josh was coming back in five days, and I was going to leave in six days. To make sure that I was going to be somewhere safe, I sent emails to four hosts in four different locations. The first to answer me were a couple living on the island of Døna, Germans who needed help with building work. I would have to travel to Helgeland, a two-day trip—thirteen hundred kilometres, travelling by bus, train, and boat.

As compensation for my translations, Josh paid me fourteen thousand krones (fifteen hundred euros). I was so grateful! For a volunteer in work exchange, this was the most money I had ever earned in two weeks. I started to believe that I really was in the richest country in all of Europe.

Now I wasn't worried about my long trips, even thought I had to pay a bit more than a thousand krones to reach the destination. I stopped at the Trondheim train station, and I was looking for hotels. They were too expensive—almost as much as my ticket—so I decided to spend the night outside. I put some of my jackets over me to cover me, and I tried to sleep on my suitcase. It was very uncomfortable, and most of the night I spent standing or walking, as it wasn't too dark. When the bus arrived at seven o'clock in the morning, I felt so tired. I wanted to sleep during my entire journey, but I had to change buses a few times and wait at the stations. The last bus brought me to Sandsjøen, and from there I took the ferry to Døna.

I hadn't made an appointment with Hans, my new host, as it was a long trip, and I couldn't be precise about the meeting time. I had his address, and it was easy to hitch-hike, as the first car I saw stopped right in front of me. The driver knew Hans and took me straight to his house.

I started to call his name as I got out of the car, and a woman appeared at the front door. She was called Alexandra, blonde with very long hair, around fifty. She was Hans's wife. I entered the house and waited inside for Hans. Alexandra knew about my arrival and had already prepared a comfortable bed for me. Wooden houses, in general, were cosy, with perfect insulation. They were easy to build, so I expected the building work to be easy to.

It was half past six in the evening when Hans arrived. He was a bit shorter than his partner, with a round, shaved head. I noticed right away that he was very funny. After dinner, he started to explain the work I was going to do with him. Hans was a professional carpenter, and my job would consist of transporting wood and cutting it with a saw. They rented the house they currently lived in, and now they were building their dream home on the coast of the other side of the island.

The next day Hans brought me to the construction site of the new house, the structure of which was already built. It stood on the rocks, held by concrete columns. That first day, I just transported the wooden planks that Hans used to cover the sides of the structure to create the walls. It was easy at the beginning, but I got tired after several hours. I didn't expect to work more than five hours, and we worked nine, with a lunch break and another shorter break in the late afternoon. At six o'clock, we left to go back to their current home.

During dinner, I opened a discussion concerning my stay, saying, 'Hans, it is a rule of work exchange that a volunteer is supposed to work five hours a day, not more.'

'Well, Martin, I didn't know about those details, but I can pay you when you pass that limit. I usually work till six o'clock, and if you agree to work till that time each day, I can pay you twelve thousand krones per month.'

'Oh! Sure, I agree! Norway is a rich country! I'm glad to be here!' I said.

'Yes, I know,' Hans said. 'Before the '70s it was one of the poorest countries in Europe. Many Norwegians emigrated to America, and that's why you see a lot of American cars around. Some of them even imported houses from there. It's crazy!'

'Then how did it become the richest country in Europe?'

'Well, Norway's economy was based on the fish market only. That's why the country was so poor. In 1971 they discovered oil, which then became its primary economy, with the fish market secondary. Now Norwegians are not too worried about making money. Some of them have a lot of money, and they prefer a simple life.'

After that good dinner, I went to my room to lie down. I wasn't feeling tired. I was happy. Now I had hope that I would have my dream of going to Bergen and learning martial arts.

It was 17 May, a national holiday in Norway. I didn't get any answer from Dag, even though I sent him two emails. This time I decided to write him a letter...

'One day, I'm gonna knock on your door, just to see if you are real or not!' I wrote.

I was crying when I wrote that phrase. I was crying for my dreams, and if I had one he was already part of it...

I spent two weeks with Hans, and everything was going well. One sunny day, we were doing roof insulation. For a moment Hans stopped and suggested that I continue without him. He went to meet a neighbour passing by. They greeted each other, and I could hear their voices from a short distance away.

'How much do you pay him?' asked the neighbour.

Hans told him, and the neighbour exclaimed, 'Twelve thousand krones?!'

'It's not too much,' Neighbour protested.

'He doesn't have papers! He's illegal,' Hans said.

'My father needs some help,' the neighbour said.

I couldn't hear anything else they said, as they were walking down the road. I felt a bit disappointed by what Hans said about me, even though it was true.

I spent my free time walking around and discovering new places. During my third week, I started to get bored, as I didn't have any other contacts. Alexandra started speaking and behaving provocatively towards me. I understood she was waiting for me to respond, but I didn't pay any attention, as it seemed she wanted to make Hans jealous. My purpose there was to make money and not to complicate people's relationships. Hans started to be colder towards me, even though I was doing a proper job and always maintained a good attitude. Of course, I had to follow some rules if I wanted to reach my goal. I didn't receive enough pay for that kind of situation. Alexandra started saying things that were not good for me. I thought she was seeking some kind of revenge for ignoring her.

During the fourth week, I felt very uncomfortable and often had headaches.

One morning, I woke up and once again asked myself, 'Where am I?'

I couldn't remember where I was. I felt lost. I got up and looked around. I gradually remembered I was in Hans's house, but I still felt foggy. For a moment I felt I was dreaming. It was a strange feeling.

I became curious to know more about this sensation that I kept experiencing, and so I started to research it on the Internet. Frightening things came up: depersonalisation, derealisation...

Oh no! I thought. *It's a syndrome! People like me see life like that...*

I went out into the forest, and I started to scream like '*The Scream*'. I became afraid. Afraid of the trees and everything. I was losing energy. I was afraid I might be losing my mind.

On the way back to the house, I saw Hans with the neighbour. They were talking, and for a moment the neighbour threw a side eye towards me and turned his back.

I went inside and waited for Hans. As it was the last day of the month, I wanted to ask for my salary.

Hans came in and opened his wallet. He left five thousand krones on the table, saying, 'Here is your salary, Martin!'

'Isn't it twelve thousand?' I asked, knowing the amount we had agreed upon.

'No, five thousand,' he said.

'That's not even half of what we agreed to!' I protested. 'Do you want to take advantage of me?'

'Keep your voice down!' Alexandra said, standing up and looking very angry.

'If I don't make a profit it's not a business for me,' continued Hans. 'You are a bit weird, you know! You stayed here for one month and never showed interest in her.'

Alexandra nodded her head.

Hans started to shake his hand and laugh.

I didn't say any more. I took the money, and I went into my room. It was over! I had to write emails to hosts nearby.

The next day, I didn't go to work. I was ready to sleep outside and wait for an answer from another host. The day after that, Hans put my suitcase outside. It was in the morning, and I was still hoping for an answer.

After six hours of waiting, someone answered me, from a small town called Røsvik. It was not too far from where I was. I took the ferry back to Sandsjøen. From there, I took the bus to my destination. It took me longer than expected, as I didn't know well the way. It was eight o'clock in the evening when I arrived at the Røsvik bus station. I sent them an email, hoping they would read it and come pick me up. After an hour, a Volkswagen Tuareg stopped nearby. An old couple smiled at me from inside the car. I immediately understood that they were my new hosts. They got out of the car to greet me, each shaking my hand. She was called Bente, and he was called Girik.

We arrived at their home, passing through a fabulous garden. I noticed two buildings. Girik explained that these served as a B & B, but my job consisted only of gardening.

After a quick dinner, Bente accompanied me to the guest house. On the first floor were a small kitchen and a living room. Upstairs were three rooms. I observed the walls, painted in different glowing colours.

'I like these colours!' I said, impressed

'I'm a colour therapist! I have been studying colours for more than thirty years,' she said.

This was the moment to ask my big question: 'What's the meaning of the colour pink?'

'It is a masculine colour, and it's the colour of *loving yourself*,' she said.

On Saturday, i was waiting for Bente inside the therapy room. As she had promised me at the beginning, she was going to offer me a colour session. My journey had meaning now, and I knew well which colour I had to choose. Bente came in, and I had already set seven different bottles on the table. The first I chose was a bottle with no colour. It was for that time when I'd lost all my feelings and felt empty.

Pale Coral/Platinum

Serenity

Bente took an old book and started to read:

> It is called *Serenity*. In these colours we find a perfect balance between enlightened masculine and Divine feminine. Serenity comes from the balance between our platinium angelic self and our magical inner starchild can play in these colours. Here we can surrender into the knowledge that finally we are whole and with that comes unconditional self acceptance and sublime serenity.

Bente then said, 'You have to know, Martin, that this colour you chose was pink before.'

Blue

Grace Under Pressure

The second colour I took was a dark blue, with a lighter blue on the top, as I still had hope. It represented the moment before leaving my country. This colour was called *Grace under pressure*.
Bente started to read again:

> This vibration carries the heaviest lessons of all. This is the path of the master. You will only do life in this way if you have chosen a path of accelerated healing and learning. This is the choice of the Olympic spiritual athlete. This path has been immeasurably difficult, but the outcome will be as magnificient as the journey was hard. No one who is not very serious about their spiritual choose this path. You are back to help humanity, to not make the same mistakes again. Clear the past karma, which is only ever based on self-judgement, and release yourself. It is now time to turn the corner and stop the suffering and reap the reward of this incredible journey. Your higher self and your angels know who you are and you are very loved and supported. Honour yourself for your choices. This has been the path of the job and you have had to lose everything to gain everything, and more. Step into grace. All the debts are paied and you are free.

Royal Blue/Olive Green

Communication

The third bottle was the green one. This was the green energy I had felt while in France. This colour was called *Communication*.

Bente read:

> Royal blue is the colour of the third eye and is about the ability to communicate your vision. Your viewpoint is very valid at the moment and whatever it is you feel you need to express will be received. Your time of been seen and not heard is over and you can now speak your truth. You also seem to carry a blue cloak of protection at the moment and this is a time to manifest your plans. The olive green in the depth allows you to base your decisions on the feminine wisdom that you carry within. Everything you touch is turning out positively at this moment.

Bente explained further, 'The third eye means that you have the ability to communicate between images, Martin.'

This was the only colour I refused.

Magenta/Copper

Awakening

The fourth colour I chose was the brown one which reminded me of food, especially Nutella. It was called *Awakening*.

Bente read:

> The awakening is the soul awakening to its true self and understanding the essential truth that there is no separation. These colours say that we never left home in the first place. As we realise that the Creator is in everything you begin to understand we are the creator in a physical form, and the copper connected to the magenta is where we begin to understand that we are bodies as souls of heaven and of earth. There is no separation and our physical forms are the link between heaven and earth. Souls and bodies are as one and we awaken when we see that truth clearly. What seems furthest removed from spirit becomes God's perfection unfolding when we see it all as God all perfect.

'Good advice to remember about this colour is that you have to grow up yourself on earth,' said Bente.

Pale Turquoise

Movement

The fifth one I chose was the blue one, also my favourite colour, which reminds me of the sea, the sky, and water. To me, it was the colour of freedom. This colour was called *Movement*.
Bente read:

> The number 14 is ruled by Mercury, communication with the public and relates to the media, publishing, television and the Internet. The unexpected can happen at any moment. Travel is in the air, good fortune is yours. Soon you will find the sanctuary your spirit calls for.

Pink

Venus

The sixth I chose was the pink one, because after finding all these colours, I found myself also. This colour was called *Venus*.
Bente read:

Venus relates to love, harmony and joy in relationships. She is feminine and brings love into our lives when we learn that love from the outside comes when we reach a place of deep self-acceptance. Pink is the colour of unconditional love and tells us that more we are able to love ourselves, the more abundant our lives will be. A feeling of "not enough" inside will lead to a reality reflection of "not enough" outside. This is also the colour we relate to the feminine side and mothering. Maybe now is the time to treat yourself to some of your own nurturing energy.

Red/Rose Pink

Spiritual and Material Conflict

The seventh I chose was the red one. This was the colour of love colour, as far as I knew, but love for someone else. After loving myself, I wanted to love someone else, of course. This colour was called *Spiritual and material conflict.*

Bente read:

> This is a difficult vibration because it denotes confusion. Notice what blocks you from bringing heaven to earth and notice when you still betray yourself by not believing that you are the "I Am". These colours are all about bringing heaven to earth, the earth being the red, the lowest vibration where we hold onto what is real. Your health, money and relationships are all the real things in your life. This is the last bit of illusion that needs to be overcome so that you might see them as part of your spiritual journey and the way back to the Allness. This bottle indicates a lifetime as a nun or a monk.

My stay at their house consisted of only two weeks, as another volunteer was going to replace me. The job was easy, cutting grass and branches and sometimes doing some planting. I felt sorry that I had to leave in such a short time, as I was enjoying those sunny days in that magical garden.

I planned to go further north, where there were fewer people and no immigrants. Hosts were looking for help, desperate and ready to pay for work. I wrote to two hosts in two different locations: Tromsø and Alta, which was even further north. The first answer came from Alta, a small town also known as Northern Sami. I wasn't going to live in the city centre, but on a farm in the countryside.

It was a long trip of fourteen hours by bus and boat. There was little chance I'd reach my destination in one day. I enjoyed the journey, though, fascinated by the landscape. I sometimes felt like I had travelled to another planet. It was ten o'clock at night when I arrived in Alta. Christian, my new host, was waiting at the bus station. He was Norwegian, around forty or a bit older. His wife was Sami, a little woman who almost looked Chinese.

'Where do you come from?' asked Christian.

I understood he wasn't the one who read my emails.

'I'm from Albania.'

'Albania! I have two Albanian friends here. One is a taxi driver, and the other is a carpenter. Both are good guys.'

In fifteen minutes we arrived at a large farmhouse. A big stable sat a distance away. Christian introduced me to his daughter and his employee from Spain who had arrived three days before.

'He's called David,' Christian said, then explained, 'We pay him, but you will stay as a volunteer and help him take care of our animals. We have goats, sheep, ducks, rabbits, and horses.'

Their daughter, Alice, was tall as her father, around twenty, and studying nursing.

I was going to sleep in a building apart from the house, the same place where David slept.

I felt hopeless the first two days I was helping David, as I noticed he was lazy. I chose to work alone.

'Martin! Can you come here, please?' David called.

He was standing in front of two Australian emus and not daring to go inside. It was the first I had seen these huge birds. I was a bit surprised, as Christian hadn't mentioned them.

'I'm afraid of them; they may bite. Can you feed them for me, please?' David said.

Alice was passing by and said, 'Pussy! Martin, go inside and show him who is a real man!'

I felt provoked, but I hesitated. I took the bucket and set it inside on the ground. Two seconds later, I turned to close the door.

Alice smiled at me as she left.

During dinner, Alice asked me how long I planned to stay and suggested some interesting things and places I could do and see.

'Down the shore we can go fishing. Sometimes whales even pass by,' said Alice.

Whales! I wanted to see a whale.

'And in late August I promise you'll see some Northern Lights,' she added.

Northern Lights! I wanted to see the Northern Lights.

I noticed David wasn't curious about anything. I went to my room and had a deep sleep, as I felt very tired.

I woke up, stood up, and went outside. It was still night and very quiet. I went down the road close to the shore. I walked slowly and i felt my feet touching the water. A string of green lights streaked through the sky. I went into the sea. I didn't feel the cold; I didn't feel anything. I was breathing underwater. Something black and massive appeared in front of me. It was a whale. She kept approaching, faster and faster. For a moment, I start to feel the water rush around me.

And then I woke up for real. It was a dream—a nightmare! I stood up and drank some water.

I noticed the blue light blinking on my phone, and I checked my emails. It was a reply from Dag...

Printed in the United States
By Bookmasters